C-4337 CAREER EXAMINATION SERIES

*This is your
PASSBOOK for...*

Pesticide Applicator

*Test Preparation Study Guide
Questions & Answers*

COPYRIGHT NOTICE

This book is SOLELY intended for, is sold ONLY to, and its use is RESTRICTED to individual, bona fide applicants or candidates who qualify by virtue of having seriously filed applications for appropriate license, certificate, professional and/or promotional advancement, higher school matriculation, scholarship, or other legitimate requirements of education and/or governmental authorities.

This book is NOT intended for use, class instruction, tutoring, training, duplication, copying, reprinting, excerption, or adaptation, etc., by:

1) Other publishers
2) Proprietors and/or Instructors of "Coaching" and/or Preparatory Courses
3) Personnel and/or Training Divisions of commercial, industrial, and governmental organizations
4) Schools, colleges, or universities and/or their departments and staffs, including teachers and other personnel
5) Testing Agencies or Bureaus
6) Study groups which seek by the purchase of a single volume to copy and/or duplicate and/or adapt this material for use by the group as a whole without having purchased individual volumes for each of the members of the group
7) Et al.

Such persons would be in violation of appropriate Federal and State statutes.

PROVISION OF LICENSING AGREEMENTS – Recognized educational, commercial, industrial, and governmental institutions and organizations, and others legitimately engaged in educational pursuits, including training, testing, and measurement activities, may address request for a licensing agreement to the copyright owners, who will determine whether, and under what conditions, including fees and charges, the materials in this book may be used them. In other words, a licensing facility exists for the legitimate use of the material in this book on other than an individual basis. However, it is asseverated and affirmed here that the material in this book CANNOT be used without the receipt of the express permission of such a licensing agreement from the Publishers. Inquiries re licensing should be addressed to the company, attention rights and permissions department.

All rights reserved, including the right of reproduction in whole or in part, in any form or by any means, electronic or mechanical, including photocopying, recording, or by any information storage and retrieval system, without permission in writing from the Publisher.

Copyright © 2024 by
National Learning Corporation

212 Michael Drive, Syosset, NY 11791
(516) 921-8888 • www.passbooks.com
E-mail: info@passbooks.com

PUBLISHED IN THE UNITED STATES OF AMERICA

PASSBOOK® SERIES

THE *PASSBOOK® SERIES* has been created to prepare applicants and candidates for the ultimate academic battlefield – the examination room.

At some time in our lives, each and every one of us may be required to take an examination – for validation, matriculation, admission, qualification, registration, certification, or licensure.

Based on the assumption that every applicant or candidate has met the basic formal educational standards, has taken the required number of courses, and read the necessary texts, the *PASSBOOK® SERIES* furnishes the one special preparation which may assure passing with confidence, instead of failing with insecurity. Examination questions – together with answers – are furnished as the basic vehicle for study so that the mysteries of the examination and its compounding difficulties may be eliminated or diminished by a sure method.

This book is meant to help you pass your examination provided that you qualify and are serious in your objective.

The entire field is reviewed through the huge store of content information which is succinctly presented through a provocative and challenging approach – the question-and-answer method.

A climate of success is established by furnishing the correct answers at the end of each test.

You soon learn to recognize types of questions, forms of questions, and patterns of questioning. You may even begin to anticipate expected outcomes.

You perceive that many questions are repeated or adapted so that you can gain acute insights, which may enable you to score many sure points.

You learn how to confront new questions, or types of questions, and to attack them confidently and work out the correct answers.

You note objectives and emphases, and recognize pitfalls and dangers, so that you may make positive educational adjustments.

Moreover, you are kept fully informed in relation to new concepts, methods, practices, and directions in the field.

You discover that you are actually taking the examination all the time: you are preparing for the examination by "taking" an examination, not by reading extraneous and/or supererogatory textbooks.

In short, this PASSBOOK®, used directedly, should be an important factor in helping you to pass your test.

PESTICIDE APPLICATOR

Commercial Certified (Occupation Licenses)

JOB DESCRIPTION

A certified pesticide applicator applies pesticide to kill pests that infest buildings, surrounding areas, and agricultural settings. The pesticide applicator applies the pesticide through chemical spraying, dusting, or spreading granular materials. The pesticide applicator may also clean areas that harbor pests, select appropriate extermination methods and chemicals, and counsel clients on prevention and control of pests. A pesticide applicator certified to work the commercial sector travels to commercial properties such as restaurants, office buildings, educational institutions, or agricultural settings. A pesticide applicator may be self-employed or operate from an established firm. A working knowledge of the occupation is necessary for examination. Applicant must pass both the written and practical examinations. Possible areas of study include pesticide laws, rules.

Non-Commercial Certified (Occupation Licenses)

A certified pesticide applicator applies pesticide to kill pests that infest buildings and surrounding areas. The pesticide applicator applies the pesticide through chemical spraying, dusting, or spreading granular materials. The pesticide applicator may also clean areas that harbor pests, select appropriate extermination methods and chemicals, and counsel clients on prevention and control of pests. A pesticide applicator certified to work non-commercially may utilize pesticides only in residences and other specified areas. A pesticide applicator may be self-employed or operate from an established firm. Possible areas of study include pesticide laws, rules, safety, pesticide use, disposal, worker protection, ground water, and endangered species.

HOW TO TAKE A TEST

I. YOU MUST PASS AN EXAMINATION

A. *WHAT EVERY CANDIDATE SHOULD KNOW*

Examination applicants often ask us for help in preparing for the written test. What can I study in advance? What kinds of questions will be asked? How will the test be given? How will the papers be graded?

As an applicant for a civil service examination, you may be wondering about some of these things. Our purpose here is to suggest effective methods of advance study and to describe civil service examinations.

Your chances for success on this examination can be increased if you know how to prepare. Those "pre-examination jitters" can be reduced if you know what to expect. You can even experience an adventure in good citizenship if you know why civil service exams are given.

B. *WHY ARE CIVIL SERVICE EXAMINATIONS GIVEN?*

Civil service examinations are important to you in two ways. As a citizen, you want public jobs filled by employees who know how to do their work. As a job seeker, you want a fair chance to compete for that job on an equal footing with other candidates. The best-known means of accomplishing this two-fold goal is the competitive examination.

Exams are widely publicized throughout the nation. They may be administered for jobs in federal, state, city, municipal, town or village governments or agencies.

Any citizen may apply, with some limitations, such as the age or residence of applicants. Your experience and education may be reviewed to see whether you meet the requirements for the particular examination. When these requirements exist, they are reasonable and applied consistently to all applicants. Thus, a competitive examination may cause you some uneasiness now, but it is your privilege and safeguard.

C. *HOW ARE CIVIL SERVICE EXAMS DEVELOPED?*

Examinations are carefully written by trained technicians who are specialists in the field known as "psychological measurement," in consultation with recognized authorities in the field of work that the test will cover. These experts recommend the subject matter areas or skills to be tested; only those knowledges or skills important to your success on the job are included. The most reliable books and source materials available are used as references. Together, the experts and technicians judge the difficulty level of the questions.

Test technicians know how to phrase questions so that the problem is clearly stated. Their ethics do not permit "trick" or "catch" questions. Questions may have been tried out on sample groups, or subjected to statistical analysis, to determine their usefulness.

Written tests are often used in combination with performance tests, ratings of training and experience, and oral interviews. All of these measures combine to form the best-known means of finding the right person for the right job.

II. HOW TO PASS THE WRITTEN TEST

A. NATURE OF THE EXAMINATION

To prepare intelligently for civil service examinations, you should know how they differ from school examinations you have taken. In school you were assigned certain definite pages to read or subjects to cover. The examination questions were quite detailed and usually emphasized memory. Civil service exams, on the other hand, try to discover your present ability to perform the duties of a position, plus your potentiality to learn these duties. In other words, a civil service exam attempts to predict how successful you will be. Questions cover such a broad area that they cannot be as minute and detailed as school exam questions.

In the public service similar kinds of work, or positions, are grouped together in one "class." This process is known as *position-classification*. All the positions in a class are paid according to the salary range for that class. One class title covers all of these positions, and they are all tested by the same examination.

B. FOUR BASIC STEPS

1) Study the announcement

How, then, can you know what subjects to study? Our best answer is: "Learn as much as possible about the class of positions for which you've applied." The exam will test the knowledge, skills and abilities needed to do the work.

Your most valuable source of information about the position you want is the official exam announcement. This announcement lists the training and experience qualifications. Check these standards and apply only if you come reasonably close to meeting them.

The brief description of the position in the examination announcement offers some clues to the subjects which will be tested. Think about the job itself. Review the duties in your mind. Can you perform them, or are there some in which you are rusty? Fill in the blank spots in your preparation.

Many jurisdictions preview the written test in the exam announcement by including a section called "Knowledge and Abilities Required," "Scope of the Examination," or some similar heading. Here you will find out specifically what fields will be tested.

2) Review your own background

Once you learn in general what the position is all about, and what you need to know to do the work, ask yourself which subjects you already know fairly well and which need improvement. You may wonder whether to concentrate on improving your strong areas or on building some background in your fields of weakness. When the announcement has specified "some knowledge" or "considerable knowledge," or has used adjectives like "beginning principles of…" or "advanced … methods," you can get a clue as to the number and difficulty of questions to be asked in any given field. More questions, and hence broader coverage, would be included for those subjects which are more important in the work. Now weigh your strengths and weaknesses against the job requirements and prepare accordingly.

3) Determine the level of the position

Another way to tell how intensively you should prepare is to understand the level of the job for which you are applying. Is it the entering level? In other words, is this the position in which beginners in a field of work are hired? Or is it an intermediate or advanced level? Sometimes this is indicated by such words as "Junior" or "Senior" in the class title. Other jurisdictions use Roman numerals to designate the level – Clerk I, Clerk II, for example. The word "Supervisor" sometimes appears in the title. If the level is not indicated by the title, check the description of duties. Will you be working under very close supervision, or will you have responsibility for independent decisions in this work?

4) Choose appropriate study materials

Now that you know the subjects to be examined and the relative amount of each subject to be covered, you can choose suitable study materials. For beginning level jobs, or even advanced ones, if you have a pronounced weakness in some aspect of your training, read a modern, standard textbook in that field. Be sure it is up to date and has general coverage. Such books are normally available at your library, and the librarian will be glad to help you locate one. For entry-level positions, questions of appropriate difficulty are chosen – neither highly advanced questions, nor those too simple. Such questions require careful thought but not advanced training.

If the position for which you are applying is technical or advanced, you will read more advanced, specialized material. If you are already familiar with the basic principles of your field, elementary textbooks would waste your time. Concentrate on advanced textbooks and technical periodicals. Think through the concepts and review difficult problems in your field.

These are all general sources. You can get more ideas on your own initiative, following these leads. For example, training manuals and publications of the government agency which employs workers in your field can be useful, particularly for technical and professional positions. A letter or visit to the government department involved may result in more specific study suggestions, and certainly will provide you with a more definite idea of the exact nature of the position you are seeking.

III. KINDS OF TESTS

Tests are used for purposes other than measuring knowledge and ability to perform specified duties. For some positions, it is equally important to test ability to make adjustments to new situations or to profit from training. In others, basic mental abilities not dependent on information are essential. Questions which test these things may not appear as pertinent to the duties of the position as those which test for knowledge and information. Yet they are often highly important parts of a fair examination. For very general questions, it is almost impossible to help you direct your study efforts. What we can do is to point out some of the more common of these general abilities needed in public service positions and describe some typical questions.

1) General information

Broad, general information has been found useful for predicting job success in some kinds of work. This is tested in a variety of ways, from vocabulary lists to questions about current events. Basic background in some field of work, such as sociology or economics, may be sampled in a group of questions. Often these are principles which have become familiar to most persons through exposure rather than through formal training. It is difficult to advise you how to study for these questions; being alert to the world around you is our best suggestion.

2) Verbal ability

An example of an ability needed in many positions is verbal or language ability. Verbal ability is, in brief, the ability to use and understand words. Vocabulary and grammar tests are typical measures of this ability. Reading comprehension or paragraph interpretation questions are common in many kinds of civil service tests. You are given a paragraph of written material and asked to find its central meaning.

3) Numerical ability

Number skills can be tested by the familiar arithmetic problem, by checking paired lists of numbers to see which are alike and which are different, or by interpreting charts and graphs. In the latter test, a graph may be printed in the test booklet which you are asked to use as the basis for answering questions.

4) Observation

A popular test for law-enforcement positions is the observation test. A picture is shown to you for several minutes, then taken away. Questions about the picture test your ability to observe both details and larger elements.

5) Following directions

In many positions in the public service, the employee must be able to carry out written instructions dependably and accurately. You may be given a chart with several columns, each column listing a variety of information. The questions require you to carry out directions involving the information given in the chart.

6) Skills and aptitudes

Performance tests effectively measure some manual skills and aptitudes. When the skill is one in which you are trained, such as typing or shorthand, you can practice. These tests are often very much like those given in business school or high school courses. For many of the other skills and aptitudes, however, no short-time preparation can be made. Skills and abilities natural to you or that you have developed throughout your lifetime are being tested.

Many of the general questions just described provide all the data needed to answer the questions and ask you to use your reasoning ability to find the answers. Your best preparation for these tests, as well as for tests of facts and ideas, is to be at your physical and mental best. You, no doubt, have your own methods of getting into an exam-taking mood and keeping "in shape." The next section lists some ideas on this subject.

IV. KINDS OF QUESTIONS

Only rarely is the "essay" question, which you answer in narrative form, used in civil service tests. Civil service tests are usually of the short-answer type. Full instructions for answering these questions will be given to you at the examination. But in case this is your first experience with short-answer questions and separate answer sheets, here is what you need to know:

1) Multiple-choice Questions

Most popular of the short-answer questions is the "multiple choice" or "best answer" question. It can be used, for example, to test for factual knowledge, ability to solve problems or judgment in meeting situations found at work.

A multiple-choice question is normally one of three types—
- It can begin with an incomplete statement followed by several possible endings. You are to find the one ending which *best* completes the statement, although some of the others may not be entirely wrong.
- It can also be a complete statement in the form of a question which is answered by choosing one of the statements listed.

- It can be in the form of a problem – again you select the best answer.

Here is an example of a multiple-choice question with a discussion which should give you some clues as to the method for choosing the right answer:

When an employee has a complaint about his assignment, the action which will *best* help him overcome his difficulty is to
   A. discuss his difficulty with his coworkers
   B. take the problem to the head of the organization
   C. take the problem to the person who gave him the assignment
   D. say nothing to anyone about his complaint

In answering this question, you should study each of the choices to find which is best. Consider choice "A" – Certainly an employee may discuss his complaint with fellow employees, but no change or improvement can result, and the complaint remains unresolved. Choice "B" is a poor choice since the head of the organization probably does not know what assignment you have been given, and taking your problem to him is known as "going over the head" of the supervisor. The supervisor, or person who made the assignment, is the person who can clarify it or correct any injustice. Choice "C" is, therefore, correct. To say nothing, as in choice "D," is unwise. Supervisors have and interest in knowing the problems employees are facing, and the employee is seeking a solution to his problem.

2) True/False Questions

The "true/false" or "right/wrong" form of question is sometimes used. Here a complete statement is given. Your job is to decide whether the statement is right or wrong.

SAMPLE: A roaming cell-phone call to a nearby city costs less than a non-roaming call to a distant city.

This statement is wrong, or false, since roaming calls are more expensive.

This is not a complete list of all possible question forms, although most of the others are variations of these common types. You will always get complete directions for answering questions. Be sure you understand *how* to mark your answers – ask questions until you do.

V. RECORDING YOUR ANSWERS

Computer terminals are used more and more today for many different kinds of exams.
For an examination with very few applicants, you may be told to record your answers in the test booklet itself. Separate answer sheets are much more common. If this separate answer sheet is to be scored by machine – and this is often the case – it is highly important that you mark your answers correctly in order to get credit.
An electronic scoring machine is often used in civil service offices because of the speed with which papers can be scored. Machine-scored answer sheets must be marked with a pencil, which will be given to you. This pencil has a high graphite content which responds to the electronic scoring machine. As a matter of fact, stray dots may register as answers, so do not let your pencil rest on the answer sheet while you are pondering the correct answer. Also, if your pencil lead breaks or is otherwise defective, ask for another.

Since the answer sheet will be dropped in a slot in the scoring machine, be careful not to bend the corners or get the paper crumpled.

The answer sheet normally has five vertical columns of numbers, with 30 numbers to a column. These numbers correspond to the question numbers in your test booklet. After each number, going across the page are four or five pairs of dotted lines. These short dotted lines have small letters or numbers above them. The first two pairs may also have a "T" or "F" above the letters. This indicates that the first two pairs only are to be used if the questions are of the true-false type. If the questions are multiple choice, disregard the "T" and "F" and pay attention only to the small letters or numbers.

Answer your questions in the manner of the sample that follows:

32. The largest city in the United States is
    A. Washington, D.C.
    B. New York City
    C. Chicago
    D. Detroit
    E. San Francisco

1) Choose the answer you think is best. (New York City is the largest, so "B" is correct.)
2) Find the row of dotted lines numbered the same as the question you are answering. (Find row number 32)
3) Find the pair of dotted lines corresponding to the answer. (Find the pair of lines under the mark "B.")
4) Make a solid black mark between the dotted lines.

VI. BEFORE THE TEST

Common sense will help you find procedures to follow to get ready for an examination. Too many of us, however, overlook these sensible measures. Indeed, nervousness and fatigue have been found to be the most serious reasons why applicants fail to do their best on civil service tests. Here is a list of reminders:

- Begin your preparation early – Don't wait until the last minute to go scurrying around for books and materials or to find out what the position is all about.
- Prepare continuously – An hour a night for a week is better than an all-night cram session. This has been definitely established. What is more, a night a week for a month will return better dividends than crowding your study into a shorter period of time.
- Locate the place of the exam – You have been sent a notice telling you when and where to report for the examination. If the location is in a different town or otherwise unfamiliar to you, it would be well to inquire the best route and learn something about the building.
- Relax the night before the test – Allow your mind to rest. Do not study at all that night. Plan some mild recreation or diversion; then go to bed early and get a good night's sleep.
- Get up early enough to make a leisurely trip to the place for the test – This way unforeseen events, traffic snarls, unfamiliar buildings, etc. will not upset you.
- Dress comfortably – A written test is not a fashion show. You will be known by number and not by name, so wear something comfortable.

- Leave excess paraphernalia at home – Shopping bags and odd bundles will get in your way. You need bring only the items mentioned in the official notice you received; usually everything you need is provided. Do not bring reference books to the exam. They will only confuse those last minutes and be taken away from you when in the test room.
- Arrive somewhat ahead of time – If because of transportation schedules you must get there very early, bring a newspaper or magazine to take your mind off yourself while waiting.
- Locate the examination room – When you have found the proper room, you will be directed to the seat or part of the room where you will sit. Sometimes you are given a sheet of instructions to read while you are waiting. Do not fill out any forms until you are told to do so; just read them and be prepared.
- Relax and prepare to listen to the instructions
- If you have any physical problem that may keep you from doing your best, be sure to tell the test administrator. If you are sick or in poor health, you really cannot do your best on the exam. You can come back and take the test some other time.

VII. AT THE TEST

The day of the test is here and you have the test booklet in your hand. The temptation to get going is very strong. Caution! There is more to success than knowing the right answers. You must know how to identify your papers and understand variations in the type of short-answer question used in this particular examination. Follow these suggestions for maximum results from your efforts:

1) Cooperate with the monitor

The test administrator has a duty to create a situation in which you can be as much at ease as possible. He will give instructions, tell you when to begin, check to see that you are marking your answer sheet correctly, and so on. He is not there to guard you, although he will see that your competitors do not take unfair advantage. He wants to help you do your best.

2) Listen to all instructions

Don't jump the gun! Wait until you understand all directions. In most civil service tests you get more time than you need to answer the questions. So don't be in a hurry. Read each word of instructions until you clearly understand the meaning. Study the examples, listen to all announcements and follow directions. Ask questions if you do not understand what to do.

3) Identify your papers

Civil service exams are usually identified by number only. You will be assigned a number; you must not put your name on your test papers. Be sure to copy your number correctly. Since more than one exam may be given, copy your exact examination title.

4) Plan your time

Unless you are told that a test is a "speed" or "rate of work" test, speed itself is usually not important. Time enough to answer all the questions will be provided, but this does not mean that you have all day. An overall time limit has been set. Divide the total time (in minutes) by the number of questions to determine the approximate time you have for each question.

5) Do not linger over difficult questions

If you come across a difficult question, mark it with a paper clip (useful to have along) and come back to it when you have been through the booklet. One caution if you do this – be sure to skip a number on your answer sheet as well. Check often to be sure that you have not lost your place and that you are marking in the row numbered the same as the question you are answering.

6) Read the questions

Be sure you know what the question asks! Many capable people are unsuccessful because they failed to *read* the questions correctly.

7) Answer all questions

Unless you have been instructed that a penalty will be deducted for incorrect answers, it is better to guess than to omit a question.

8) Speed tests

It is often better NOT to guess on speed tests. It has been found that on timed tests people are tempted to spend the last few seconds before time is called in marking answers at random – without even reading them – in the hope of picking up a few extra points. To discourage this practice, the instructions may warn you that your score will be "corrected" for guessing. That is, a penalty will be applied. The incorrect answers will be deducted from the correct ones, or some other penalty formula will be used.

9) Review your answers

If you finish before time is called, go back to the questions you guessed or omitted to give them further thought. Review other answers if you have time.

10) Return your test materials

If you are ready to leave before others have finished or time is called, take ALL your materials to the monitor and leave quietly. Never take any test material with you. The monitor can discover whose papers are not complete, and taking a test booklet may be grounds for disqualification.

VIII. EXAMINATION TECHNIQUES

1) Read the general instructions carefully. These are usually printed on the first page of the exam booklet. As a rule, these instructions refer to the timing of the examination; the fact that you should not start work until the signal and must stop work at a signal, etc. If there are any *special* instructions, such as a choice of questions to be answered, make sure that you note this instruction carefully.

2) When you are ready to start work on the examination, that is as soon as the signal has been given, read the instructions to each question booklet, underline any key words or phrases, such as *least, best, outline, describe* and the like. In this way you will tend to answer as requested rather than discover on reviewing your paper that you *listed without describing*, that you selected the *worst* choice rather than the *best* choice, etc.

3) If the examination is of the objective or multiple-choice type – that is, each question will also give a series of possible answers: A, B, C or D, and you are called upon to select the best answer and write the letter next to that answer on your answer paper – it is advisable to start answering each question in turn. There may be anywhere from 50 to 100 such questions in the three or four hours allotted and you can see how much time would be taken if you read through all the questions before beginning to answer any. Furthermore, if you come across a question or group of questions which you know would be difficult to answer, it would undoubtedly affect your handling of all the other questions.

4) If the examination is of the essay type and contains but a few questions, it is a moot point as to whether you should read all the questions before starting to answer any one. Of course, if you are given a choice – say five out of seven and the like – then it is essential to read all the questions so you can eliminate the two that are most difficult. If, however, you are asked to answer all the questions, there may be danger in trying to answer the easiest one first because you may find that you will spend too much time on it. The best technique is to answer the first question, then proceed to the second, etc.

5) Time your answers. Before the exam begins, write down the time it started, then add the time allowed for the examination and write down the time it must be completed, then divide the time available somewhat as follows:
    - If 3-1/2 hours are allowed, that would be 210 minutes. If you have 80 objective-type questions, that would be an average of 2-1/2 minutes per question. Allow yourself no more than 2 minutes per question, or a total of 160 minutes, which will permit about 50 minutes to review.
    - If for the time allotment of 210 minutes there are 7 essay questions to answer, that would average about 30 minutes a question. Give yourself only 25 minutes per question so that you have about 35 minutes to review.

6) The most important instruction is to *read each question* and make sure you know what is wanted. The second most important instruction is to *time yourself properly* so that you answer every question. The third most important instruction is to *answer every question*. Guess if you have to but include something for each question. Remember that you will receive no credit for a blank and will probably receive some credit if you write something in answer to an essay question. If you guess a letter – say "B" for a multiple-choice question – you may have guessed right. If you leave a blank as an answer to a multiple-choice question, the examiners may respect your feelings but it will not add a point to your score. Some exams may penalize you for wrong answers, so in such cases *only*, you may not want to guess unless you have some basis for your answer.

7) Suggestions
   a. Objective-type questions
      1. Examine the question booklet for proper sequence of pages and questions
      2. Read all instructions carefully
      3. Skip any question which seems too difficult; return to it after all other questions have been answered
      4. Apportion your time properly; do not spend too much time on any single question or group of questions

5. Note and underline key words – *all, most, fewest, least, best, worst, same, opposite,* etc.
6. Pay particular attention to negatives
7. Note unusual option, e.g., unduly long, short, complex, different or similar in content to the body of the question
8. Observe the use of "hedging" words – *probably, may, most likely,* etc.
9. Make sure that your answer is put next to the same number as the question
10. Do not second-guess unless you have good reason to believe the second answer is definitely more correct
11. Cross out original answer if you decide another answer is more accurate; do not erase until you are ready to hand your paper in
12. Answer all questions; guess unless instructed otherwise
13. Leave time for review

   b. Essay questions
     1. Read each question carefully
     2. Determine exactly what is wanted. Underline key words or phrases.
     3. Decide on outline or paragraph answer
     4. Include many different points and elements unless asked to develop any one or two points or elements
     5. Show impartiality by giving pros and cons unless directed to select one side only
     6. Make and write down any assumptions you find necessary to answer the questions
     7. Watch your English, grammar, punctuation and choice of words
     8. Time your answers; don't crowd material

8) Answering the essay question

Most essay questions can be answered by framing the specific response around several key words or ideas. Here are a few such key words or ideas:

M's: manpower, materials, methods, money, management
P's: purpose, program, policy, plan, procedure, practice, problems, pitfalls, personnel, public relations

   a. Six basic steps in handling problems:
     1. Preliminary plan and background development
     2. Collect information, data and facts
     3. Analyze and interpret information, data and facts
     4. Analyze and develop solutions as well as make recommendations
     5. Prepare report and sell recommendations
     6. Install recommendations and follow up effectiveness

   b. Pitfalls to avoid
     1. *Taking things for granted* – A statement of the situation does not necessarily imply that each of the elements is necessarily true; for example, a complaint may be invalid and biased so that all that can be taken for granted is that a complaint has been registered

2. *Considering only one side of a situation* – Wherever possible, indicate several alternatives and then point out the reasons you selected the best one
3. *Failing to indicate follow up* – Whenever your answer indicates action on your part, make certain that you will take proper follow-up action to see how successful your recommendations, procedures or actions turn out to be
4. *Taking too long in answering any single question* – Remember to time your answers properly

IX. AFTER THE TEST

Scoring procedures differ in detail among civil service jurisdictions although the general principles are the same. Whether the papers are hand-scored or graded by machine we have described, they are nearly always graded by number. That is, the person who marks the paper knows only the number – never the name – of the applicant. Not until all the papers have been graded will they be matched with names. If other tests, such as training and experience or oral interview ratings have been given, scores will be combined. Different parts of the examination usually have different weights. For example, the written test might count 60 percent of the final grade, and a rating of training and experience 40 percent. In many jurisdictions, veterans will have a certain number of points added to their grades.

After the final grade has been determined, the names are placed in grade order and an eligible list is established. There are various methods for resolving ties between those who get the same final grade – probably the most common is to place first the name of the person whose application was received first. Job offers are made from the eligible list in the order the names appear on it. You will be notified of your grade and your rank as soon as all these computations have been made. This will be done as rapidly as possible.

People who are found to meet the requirements in the announcement are called "eligibles." Their names are put on a list of eligible candidates. An eligible's chances of getting a job depend on how high he stands on this list and how fast agencies are filling jobs from the list.

When a job is to be filled from a list of eligibles, the agency asks for the names of people on the list of eligibles for that job. When the civil service commission receives this request, it sends to the agency the names of the three people highest on this list. Or, if the job to be filled has specialized requirements, the office sends the agency the names of the top three persons who meet these requirements from the general list.

The appointing officer makes a choice from among the three people whose names were sent to him. If the selected person accepts the appointment, the names of the others are put back on the list to be considered for future openings.

That is the rule in hiring from all kinds of eligible lists, whether they are for typist, carpenter, chemist, or something else. For every vacancy, the appointing officer has his choice of any one of the top three eligibles on the list. This explains why the person whose name is on top of the list sometimes does not get an appointment when some of the persons lower on the list do. If the appointing officer chooses the second or third eligible, the No. 1 eligible does not get a job at once, but stays on the list until he is appointed or the list is terminated.

X. HOW TO PASS THE INTERVIEW TEST

The examination for which you applied requires an oral interview test. You have already taken the written test and you are now being called for the interview test – the final part of the formal examination.

You may think that it is not possible to prepare for an interview test and that there are no procedures to follow during an interview. Our purpose is to point out some things you can do in advance that will help you and some good rules to follow and pitfalls to avoid while you are being interviewed.

What is an interview supposed to test?

The written examination is designed to test the technical knowledge and competence of the candidate; the oral is designed to evaluate intangible qualities, not readily measured otherwise, and to establish a list showing the relative fitness of each candidate – as measured against his competitors – for the position sought. Scoring is not on the basis of "right" and "wrong," but on a sliding scale of values ranging from "not passable" to "outstanding." As a matter of fact, it is possible to achieve a relatively low score without a single "incorrect" answer because of evident weakness in the qualities being measured.

Occasionally, an examination may consist entirely of an oral test – either an individual or a group oral. In such cases, information is sought concerning the technical knowledges and abilities of the candidate, since there has been no written examination for this purpose. More commonly, however, an oral test is used to supplement a written examination.

Who conducts interviews?

The composition of oral boards varies among different jurisdictions. In nearly all, a representative of the personnel department serves as chairman. One of the members of the board may be a representative of the department in which the candidate would work. In some cases, "outside experts" are used, and, frequently, a businessman or some other representative of the general public is asked to serve. Labor and management or other special groups may be represented. The aim is to secure the services of experts in the appropriate field.

However the board is composed, it is a good idea (and not at all improper or unethical) to ascertain in advance of the interview who the members are and what groups they represent. When you are introduced to them, you will have some idea of their backgrounds and interests, and at least you will not stutter and stammer over their names.

What should be done before the interview?

While knowledge about the board members is useful and takes some of the surprise element out of the interview, there is other preparation which is more substantive. It *is* possible to prepare for an oral interview – in several ways:

1) Keep a copy of your application and review it carefully before the interview

This may be the only document before the oral board, and the starting point of the interview. Know what education and experience you have listed there, and the sequence and dates of all of it. Sometimes the board will ask you to review the highlights of your experience for them; you should not have to hem and haw doing it.

2) Study the class specification and the examination announcement

Usually, the oral board has one or both of these to guide them. The qualities, characteristics or knowledges required by the position sought are stated in these documents. They offer valuable clues as to the nature of the oral interview. For example, if the job involves supervisory responsibilities, the announcement will usually indicate that knowledge of modern supervisory methods and the qualifications of the candidate as a supervisor will be tested. If so, you can expect such questions, frequently in the form of a hypothetical situation which you are expected to solve. NEVER go into an oral without knowledge of the duties and responsibilities of the job you seek.

3) Think through each qualification required

Try to visualize the kind of questions you would ask if you were a board member. How well could you answer them? Try especially to appraise your own knowledge and background in each area, *measured against the job sought*, and identify any areas in which you are weak. Be critical and realistic – do not flatter yourself.

4) Do some general reading in areas in which you feel you may be weak

For example, if the job involves supervision and your past experience has NOT, some general reading in supervisory methods and practices, particularly in the field of human relations, might be useful. Do NOT study agency procedures or detailed manuals. The oral board will be testing your understanding and capacity, not your memory.

5) Get a good night's sleep and watch your general health and mental attitude

You will want a clear head at the interview. Take care of a cold or any other minor ailment, and of course, no hangovers.

What should be done on the day of the interview?

Now comes the day of the interview itself. Give yourself plenty of time to get there. Plan to arrive somewhat ahead of the scheduled time, particularly if your appointment is in the fore part of the day. If a previous candidate fails to appear, the board might be ready for you a bit early. By early afternoon an oral board is almost invariably behind schedule if there are many candidates, and you may have to wait. Take along a book or magazine to read, or your application to review, but leave any extraneous material in the waiting room when you go in for your interview. In any event, relax and compose yourself.

The matter of dress is important. The board is forming impressions about you – from your experience, your manners, your attitude, and your appearance. Give your personal appearance careful attention. Dress your best, but not your flashiest. Choose conservative, appropriate clothing, and be sure it is immaculate. This is a business interview, and your appearance should indicate that you regard it as such. Besides, being well groomed and properly dressed will help boost your confidence.

Sooner or later, someone will call your name and escort you into the interview room. *This is it*. From here on you are on your own. It is too late for any more preparation. But remember, you asked for this opportunity to prove your fitness, and you are here because your request was granted.

What happens when you go in?

The usual sequence of events will be as follows: The clerk (who is often the board stenographer) will introduce you to the chairman of the oral board, who will introduce you to the other members of the board. Acknowledge the introductions before you sit down. Do not be surprised if you find a microphone facing you or a stenotypist sitting by. Oral interviews are usually recorded in the event of an appeal or other review.

Usually the chairman of the board will open the interview by reviewing the highlights of your education and work experience from your application – primarily for the benefit of the other members of the board, as well as to get the material into the record. Do not interrupt or comment unless there is an error or significant misinterpretation; if that is the case, do not hesitate. But do not quibble about insignificant matters. Also, he will usually ask you some question about your education, experience or your present job – partly to get you to start talking and to establish the interviewing "rapport." He may start the actual questioning, or turn it over to one of the other members. Frequently, each member undertakes the questioning on a particular area, one in which he is perhaps most competent, so you can expect each member to participate in the examination. Because time is limited, you may also expect some rather abrupt switches in the direction the questioning takes, so do not be upset by it. Normally, a board member will not pursue a single line of questioning unless he discovers a particular strength or weakness.

After each member has participated, the chairman will usually ask whether any member has any further questions, then will ask you if you have anything you wish to add. Unless you are expecting this question, it may floor you. Worse, it may start you off on an extended, extemporaneous speech. The board is not usually seeking more information. The question is principally to offer you a last opportunity to present further qualifications or to indicate that you have nothing to add. So, if you feel that a significant qualification or characteristic has been overlooked, it is proper to point it out in a sentence or so. Do not compliment the board on the thoroughness of their examination – they have been sketchy, and you know it. If you wish, merely say, "No thank you, I have nothing further to add." This is a point where you can "talk yourself out" of a good impression or fail to present an important bit of information. Remember, *you close the interview yourself*.

The chairman will then say, "That is all, Mr. _____, thank you." Do not be startled; the interview is over, and quicker than you think. Thank him, gather your belongings and take your leave. Save your sigh of relief for the other side of the door.

How to put your best foot forward

Throughout this entire process, you may feel that the board individually and collectively is trying to pierce your defenses, seek out your hidden weaknesses and embarrass and confuse you. Actually, this is not true. They are obliged to make an appraisal of your qualifications for the job you are seeking, and they want to see you in your best light. Remember, they must interview all candidates and a non-cooperative candidate may become a failure in spite of their best efforts to bring out his qualifications. Here are 15 suggestions that will help you:

1) Be natural – Keep your attitude confident, not cocky

If you are not confident that you can do the job, do not expect the board to be. Do not apologize for your weaknesses, try to bring out your strong points. The board is interested in a positive, not negative, presentation. Cockiness will antagonize any board member and make him wonder if you are covering up a weakness by a false show of strength.

2) Get comfortable, but don't lounge or sprawl

Sit erectly but not stiffly. A careless posture may lead the board to conclude that you are careless in other things, or at least that you are not impressed by the importance of the occasion. Either conclusion is natural, even if incorrect. Do not fuss with your clothing, a pencil or an ashtray. Your hands may occasionally be useful to emphasize a point; do not let them become a point of distraction.

3) Do not wisecrack or make small talk

This is a serious situation, and your attitude should show that you consider it as such. Further, the time of the board is limited – they do not want to waste it, and neither should you.

4) Do not exaggerate your experience or abilities
   In the first place, from information in the application or other interviews and sources, the board may know more about you than you think. Secondly, you probably will not get away with it. An experienced board is rather adept at spotting such a situation, so do not take the chance.

5) If you know a board member, do not make a point of it, yet do not hide it
   Certainly you are not fooling him, and probably not the other members of the board. Do not try to take advantage of your acquaintanceship – it will probably do you little good.

6) Do not dominate the interview
   Let the board do that. They will give you the clues – do not assume that you have to do all the talking. Realize that the board has a number of questions to ask you, and do not try to take up all the interview time by showing off your extensive knowledge of the answer to the first one.

7) Be attentive
   You only have 20 minutes or so, and you should keep your attention at its sharpest throughout. When a member is addressing a problem or question to you, give him your undivided attention. Address your reply principally to him, but do not exclude the other board members.

8) Do not interrupt
   A board member may be stating a problem for you to analyze. He will ask you a question when the time comes. Let him state the problem, and wait for the question.

9) Make sure you understand the question
   Do not try to answer until you are sure what the question is. If it is not clear, restate it in your own words or ask the board member to clarify it for you. However, do not haggle about minor elements.

10) Reply promptly but not hastily
   A common entry on oral board rating sheets is "candidate responded readily," or "candidate hesitated in replies." Respond as promptly and quickly as you can, but do not jump to a hasty, ill-considered answer.

11) Do not be peremptory in your answers
   A brief answer is proper – but do not fire your answer back. That is a losing game from your point of view. The board member can probably ask questions much faster than you can answer them.

12) Do not try to create the answer you think the board member wants
   He is interested in what kind of mind you have and how it works – not in playing games. Furthermore, he can usually spot this practice and will actually grade you down on it.

13) Do not switch sides in your reply merely to agree with a board member
   Frequently, a member will take a contrary position merely to draw you out and to see if you are willing and able to defend your point of view. Do not start a debate, yet do not surrender a good position. If a position is worth taking, it is worth defending.

14) Do not be afraid to admit an error in judgment if you are shown to be wrong

The board knows that you are forced to reply without any opportunity for careful consideration. Your answer may be demonstrably wrong. If so, admit it and get on with the interview.

15) Do not dwell at length on your present job

The opening question may relate to your present assignment. Answer the question but do not go into an extended discussion. You are being examined for a *new* job, not your present one. As a matter of fact, try to phrase ALL your answers in terms of the job for which you are being examined.

Basis of Rating

Probably you will forget most of these "do's" and "don'ts" when you walk into the oral interview room. Even remembering them all will not ensure you a passing grade. Perhaps you did not have the qualifications in the first place. But remembering them will help you to put your best foot forward, without treading on the toes of the board members.

Rumor and popular opinion to the contrary notwithstanding, an oral board wants you to make the best appearance possible. They know you are under pressure – but they also want to see how you respond to it as a guide to what your reaction would be under the pressures of the job you seek. They will be influenced by the degree of poise you display, the personal traits you show and the manner in which you respond.

ABOUT THIS BOOK

This book contains tests divided into Examination Sections. Go through each test, answering every question in the margin. We have also attached a sample answer sheet at the back of the book that can be removed and used. At the end of each test look at the answer key and check your answers. On the ones you got wrong, look at the right answer choice and learn. Do not fill in the answers first. Do not memorize the questions and answers, but understand the answer and principles involved. On your test, the questions will likely be different from the samples. Questions are changed and new ones added. If you understand these past questions you should have success with any changes that arise. Tests may consist of several types of questions. We have additional books on each subject should more study be advisable or necessary for you. Finally, the more you study, the better prepared you will be. This book is intended to be the last thing you study before you walk into the examination room. Prior study of relevant texts is also recommended. NLC publishes some of these in our Fundamental Series. Knowledge and good sense are important factors in passing your exam. Good luck also helps. So now study this Passbook, absorb the material contained within and take that knowledge into the examination. Then do your best to pass that exam.

EXAMINATION SECTION

SAMPLE QUESTIONS
TEST 1
GENERAL KNOWLEDGE

DIRECTIONS: Each question or incomplete statement is followed by several suggested answers or completions. Select the one that BEST answers the question or completes the statement. *PRINT THE LETTER OF THE CORRECT ANSWER IN THE SPACE AT THE RIGHT.*

1. An example of an insect predator is the   1.____
   A. termite   B. bumblebee   C. grasshopper   D. doodlebug

2. The insect with the longest life cycle is the   2.____
   A. praying mantis   B. cicada   C. honeybee   D. termite

3. A high population density in fruit fly populations results in a(n)   3.____
   A. sharp rise in lethal mutations
   B. reduction in the number of eggs produced by females
   C. increase of male fertility
   D. weeding out of sterile flies

4. Which one of the following transmits the disease typhus?   4.____
   A. Common housefly   B. Body louse
   C. Wood tick   D. Aedes mosquito

5. The disease NOT caused by the bite of an insect is   5.____
   A. typhus   B. tetanus   C. malaria   D. yellow fever

6. A useful insect is the   6.____
   A. praying mantis   B. potato beetle
   C. cabbage butterfly   D. garden spider

7. A good place to get a supply of paramecia for culturing in the laboratory is in   7.____
   A. a running stream   B. a stagnant pond
   C. brackish water   D. the Hudson River

KEY (CORRECT ANSWERS)

1. D
2. B
3. A
4. B
5. B
6. A
7. B

TEST 2

ARITHMETICAL COMPUTATIONS

DIRECTIONS: Each question or incomplete statement is followed by several suggested answers or completions. Select the one that BEST answers the question or completes the statement. *PRINT THE LETTER OF THE CORRECT ANSWER IN THE SPACE AT THE RIGHT.*

1. When 60,987 is added to 27,835, the result is 1.____
   A. 80,712   B. 80,822   C. 87,712   D. 88,822

2. The sum of 693 + 787 + 946 + 355 + 731 is 2.____
   A. 3,512   B. 3,502   C. 3,412   D. 3,402

3. When 2,586 is subtracted from 3,003, the result is 3.____
   A. 417   B. 527   C. 1,417   D. 1,527

4. When 1.32 is subtracted from 52.6, the result is 4.____
   A. 3.94   B. 5.128   C. 39.4   D. 51.28

5. When 56 is multiplied by 438, the result is 5.____
   A. 840   B. 4,818   C. 24,528   D. 48,180

6. When 8.7 is multiplied by .34, the result is MOST NEARLY 6.____
   A. 2.9   B. 3.0   C. 29.5   D. 29.6

7. When 2 is divided by 2/3, the result is 7.____
   A. 1/3   B. 3/4   C. 1 1/3   D. 3

KEY (CORRECT ANSWERS)

1. D
2. A
3. A
4. D
5. C
6. B
7. B

TEST 3

FOLLOWING INSTRUCTIONS

DIRECTIONS: Each question or incomplete statement is followed by several suggested answers or completions. Select the one that BEST answers the question or completes the statement. *PRINT THE LETTER OF THE CORRECT ANSWER IN THE SPACE AT THE RIGHT.*

1. Look at the letters below. Draw a circle around the letter that comes first in the alphabet.
    E G D Z B F

    1.____

2. Draw a line under the odd number below that is more than 7 but less than 10.
    8 10 5 5 11 9

    2.____

3. Divide the number 16 by 4 and write your answer on the line below.

    _____

    3.____

4. If in any week Wednesday comes before Tuesday, write the number 15 on the line below. If not, write the number 18.

    _____

    4.____

5. Count the number of B's in the line below and write that number at the end of the line.
    A D A E B D C A_____

    5.____

    _____

KEY (CORRECT ANSWERS)

1. B
2. 9
3. 4
4. 18
5. 1

TEST 4

PUBLIC RELATIONS

DIRECTIONS: Each question or incomplete statement is followed by several suggested answers or completions. Select the one that BEST answers the question or completes the statement. *PRINT THE LETTER OF THE CORRECT ANSWER IN THE SPACE AT THE RIGHT.*

1. Suppose that you have been asked to answer a letter from a local board of trade requesting certain information. You find that you cannot grant this request. Of the following ways of beginning your answering letter, the BEST way is to begin by
    A. quoting the laws or regulations which forbid the release of this information
    B. stating that you are sorry that the request cannot be granted
    C. explaining in detail the reasons for your decision
    D. commending the organization for its service to the community

    1.____

2. The public is MOST likely to judge personnel largely on the basis of their
    A. experience
    B. training and experience
    C. civic mindedness
    D. manner and appearance while on duty

    2.____

3. In a governmental agency, the BASIC objective of being directly concerned with public relations should be to
    A. promote the most efficient administration of the agency
    B. reduce annual reports which will be acceptable to the public
    C. increase the size of the agency
    D. broaden the "scope and activities" of the agency

    3.____

4. Which of the following has the LEAST effect on a city department's public relations?
    A. Fluctuations in employment
    B. Amount of budget
    C. Organization plan of department
    D. Size of department

    4.____

5. The MAIN advantage for good sound public relations is to
    A. build up a good feeling and understanding between the department and the public
    B. gain public support for wage increases and better work conditions
    C. increase public interest in building projects
    D. attain a friendly and sympathetic press

    5.____

6. In dealing with the public, it is helpful to know that generally most people are more willing to do that for which they
    A. are not responsible
    B. understand the reason
    C. will be given a little assistance
    D. must learn a new skill

    6.____

KEY (CORRECT ANSWERS)

1. B
2. D
3. A
4. C
5. A
6. B

EXAMINATION SECTION
TEST 1

DIRECTIONS: Each question or incomplete statement is followed by several suggested answers or completions. Select the one that BEST answers the question or completes the statement. *PRINT THE LETTER OF THE CORRECT ANSWER IN THE SPACE AT THE RIGHT.*

Questions 1-20.

DIRECTIONS: Questions 1 through 20 are to be answered SOLELY on the basis of the information contained in the following passage, the CREW CHIEF'S REPORT, and the HEALTH INSPECTOR'S REPORT.

Block 421 is located in a heavily industrialized part of the city. There are eight six-story apartment buildings on the block. Each of these apartment buildings contains 24 five-room apartments.

When a child living in one of the apartment buildings on block 421 needs medical care, he is taken to the privately-owned child clinic a few blocks away. Dr. Stone, the director of the clinic, recently learned that 25 of the 40 children treated by his clinic for rat bites within the past year lived on block 421 at the time they were bitten. He was so concerned about the conditions on that block that he wrote a letter to the Department of Health requesting that a pest control team be sent there to help reduce the rodent threat to children living on block 421.

In response to Dr. Stone"s letter, a team of 20 pest control workers under the supervision of a crew chief named John Angelo was sent to work on block 421. They remained there for a period of four weeks. During the first week, the pest control workers cleared the garbage from the streets and backyards of the block while the crew chief inspected all of the apartment buildings there to deter-mine the extent of the rodent infestation. The crew chief and his staff spent the second week cleaning up the basements, halls, and stairs of each apartment building on the block and filling in whatever rat holes they found there. During the third week, they placed rat poison in the basements and apartments of each building. They spent the fourth week instructing the tenants of block 421 on how to keep their apartments clean of rats. Just before they left the block for the last time, Mr. Angelo placed a sign in the lobby of each apartment house which gave the name, address, and telephone number of the director of the nearest rodent control office. All of the tenants were urged to phone this number if the problem with rodents developed again.

After three months had passed and nobody from block 421 called the rodent control office to complain of a rat problem, the health department concluded that rodents were no longer a problem on block 421 and they concentrated their efforts elsewhere. Then they received a letter from Dr. Stone which said that children living on block 421 were coming to the clinic with rat bites again. He demanded that the health department conduct a follow-up inspection to determine just how successful they had been in removing rats from the block.

In response to Dr. Stone's second letter, a health inspector named Harry Rosen was sent to block 421 to make a follow-up inspection. He discovered that the block showed as many signs of rodent infestation as it had when the pest control team had first inspected the block, prior to cleaning it up. Mr. Rosen recommended that a second pest control team be sent to block 421 and that a more intensive community education program be conducted after the block was once again cleaned up and the rodents were once again removed.

2 (#1)

Reports were prepared by both the crew chief and the health inspector concerning their inspection of block 421. Copies of each of these reports labeled the CREW CHIEF'S REPORT and the HEALTH INSPECTOR'S REPORT follow.

CREW CHIEF'S REPORT

DATE INSPECTION COMPLETED: <u>August 17</u>   PREPARED BY: <u>John Angelo, Crew Chief</u>

BLOCK INSPECTED: <u>421</u>

Bldg. Address	No. of Apts. Needing Exterminating;	Conditions Found in Public Areas	Conditions Found in Apartments
5 Pier St.	12	Halls and stairs badly littered. Rat burrows in backyard.	Kitchen floors food stained. Rat holes in baseboards.
11 Pier St.	7	Basement entrance blocked by debris. Rat droppings in basement.	Uncovered garbage in kitchens. Garbage frequently thrown out windows.
6 Water Rd.	20	Holes in basement floors need filling. Rat holes behind boiler.	Rat droppings in foyers. Uncovered garbage in kitchens.
10 Water Rd.	14	Rat droppings in basement. Dead rats spotted in basement.	Kitchen floors food stained. Rat holes in baseboards.
5 Bay Rd.	4	Fire escapes littered. Backyard filled with sewage due to backun.	Garbage frequently thrown out windows. Uncovered garbage in kitchens.
9 Bay Rd.	24	Basement entrance blocked by debris. Rat holes behind boiler.	Uncovered food containers on counters. Kitchen floors food stained.
10 Canal St.	10	Rat droppings in basement. Halls and stairs badly littered.	Rat holes in baseboards. Uncovered garbage in Kitchen
14 Canal St.	14	Rat tracks seen in bacKyard. Basement entrance blocked bv debris.	Rat holes in baseboards. Uncovered food containers on counters.

HEALTH INSPECTOR'S REPORT

DATE INSPECTION COMPLETED: <u>April 17</u>   PREPARED <u>BY</u>: <u>Harry Rosen, Health Inspector</u>

BLOCK INSPECTED: <u>421</u>

Bldg. Address	No. of Apts. Needing Exterminating	Conditions Found in Public Areas	Conditions Found in Apartments
5 Pier St.	8	Rat droppings in basement. Basement entrance blocked by debris.	Rat holes in baseboards. Uncovered garbage in kitchens.
11 Pier St.	12	Rat holes behind boiler. Holes in basement floor need filling.	Rat holes in baseboards. Kitchen floors food stained.
6 Water Rd.	24	Rat holes behind boiler. Halls and stairs badly littered.	Holes in kitchen walls behind sink. Rat holes in baseboards.
10 Water Rd.	14	Basement entrance blocked by debris. Traces of old rat bait found in cellar.	Garbage frequently thrown out windows. Uncovered garbage in kitchens.
5 Bay Rd.	6	Rat droppings in basement. Dead rats found in basement.	Holes in kitchen walls behind sink. Rat droppings in foyers.
9 Bay Rd.	17	Basement entrance blocked by debris. Fire escapes littered.	Rat holes in baseboards. Uncovered food containers on counters.
10 Canal St.	14	Entrance to building badly littered. Rat holes behind boiler.	Kitchen floors food stained. Uncovered garbage in kitchens.
14 Canal St.	21	Rat droppings in basement. Halls and stairs badly littered.	Garbage frequently thrown; out windows. Rat holes in baseboards.

1. The total number of apartments on block 421 is

    A. 144 B. 192 C. 960 D. 1152

2. When children living on block 421 need health care, they are taken to the

    A. child clinic B. family doctor
    C. Health Department D. hospital

3. Pest control workers were sent to block 421 because

    A. the block is in a highly industrialized part of the city
    B. numerous tenants complained of rodent infestation on the block
    C. Dr. Stone asked that they be sent there
    D. forty children living on that block had been bitten by rats

4. The pest control workers left block 421 after they had been working there for _____ week(s).

    A. one   B. two   C. three   D. four

5. An inspection of the buildings on block 421 was INITIALLY made by
   - A. Dr. Stone
   - B. a pest control worker
   - C. Harry Rosen
   - D. John Angelo

6. In treating the rodent-infested buildings on block 421, the pest control workers placed rat poison
   - A. in basements and apartments
   - B. in building lobbies
   - C. in halls and on stairs
   - D. on streets and in backyards

7. Just before they left block 421, the pest control workers
   - A. cleared the buildings and surrounding areas of garbage
   - B. placed rat bait wherever it was needed
   - C. placed a sign in the lobby of each building
   - D. told the tenants how they could keep their apartments clean

8. After the pest control team finished its job, the Health Department thought that block 421 was clean of rodents because
   - A. they had received no further complaints from Dr. Stone
   - B. they had received no complaints from the tenants who lived there
   - C. no more children on the block were being bitten by rodents
   - D. a follow-up inspection had found no further evidence of rodents there

9. When a health inspector from the Department of Health conducted a follow-up inspection of block 421, he learned that
   - A. the block was still rat infested
   - B. the block was now free of rodents
   - C. all of the buildings now had their own exterminators
   - D. some of the buildings had been abandoned

10. The health inspector who conducted the follow-up inspection recommended that
    - A. the building owners hire their own exterminators
    - B. a second pest control team be sent to work on block 421
    - C. block 421 needed no further pest control work
    - D. all of the buildings on block 421 be demolished

11. The health inspector found the largest number of apartments needing exterminating in the building at
    - A. 6 Water Road
    - B. 10 Water Road
    - C. 9 Bay Road
    - D. 14 Canal Street

12. In which of the following buildings did the crew chief find the fewest number of apartments needing exterminating?
    - A. 5 Pier Street
    - B. 11 Pier Street
    - C. 9 Bay Road
    - D. 10 Canal Street

13. In which of the following buildings did Harry Rosen find food stained kitchen floors? 13._____

   A. 5 Pier Street B. 6 Water Road
   C. 9 Bay Road D. 10 Canal Street

14. In which of the following buildings did John Angelo find the basement entrance blocked 14._____
   by debris?

   A. 5 Pier Street B. 10 Water Road
   C. 9 Bay Road D. 10 Canal Street

15. In which of the following buildings did the health inspector find littered fire escapes? 15._____

   A. 11 Pier Street B. 6 Water Road
   C. 5 Bay Road D. 9 Bay Road

16. Harry Rosen found rat holes in the baseboards of apartments in all of the following build- 16._____
   ings EXCEPT

   A. 5 Pier Street B. 10 Water Road
   C. 9 Bay Road D. 14 Canal Street

17. How much time passed between the time the crew chief completed his inspection and 17._____
   the time the health inspector completed his?

   A. 4 weeks   B. 4 months   C. 6 months   D. 8 months

18. The only building in which both Harry Rosen and John Angelo found 14 apartments 18._____
   needing extermination was

   A. 11 Pier Street B. 10 Water Road
   C. 10 Canal Street D. 14 Canal Street

19. The total number of apartments which the crew chief found in need of exterminating was 19._____

   A. 76   B. 87   C. 105   D. 116

20. The building in which Harry Rosen found 12 apartments needing exterminating was 20._____

   A. 5 Pier Street B. 11 Pier Street
   C. 6 Water Road D. 14 Canal Street

KEY (CORRECT ANSWERS)

1.	B	11.	A
2.	A	12.	B
3.	C	13.	D
4.	D	14.	C
5.	D	15.	D
6.	A	16.	B
7.	C	17.	D
8.	B	18.	B
9.	A	19.	C
10.	B	20.	B

TEST 2

DIRECTIONS: Each question or incomplete statement is followed by several suggested answers or completions. Select the one that BEST answers the question or completes the statement. *PRINT THE LETTER OF THE CORRECT ANSWER IN THE SPACE AT THE RIGHT.*

Questions 1-10.

DIRECTIONS: Questions 1 through 10 are to be answered SOLELY on the basis of the information contained in the following passage and refer to entries that would be made on the FIELD VISIT REPORT form that follows the passage.

On March 6, a crew composed of five Community Service Aides and three Pest Control Aides, under the supervision of a Crew Chief (Pest Control), made a field visit to inspect several residential buildings and a vacant lot. The purpose of the visit was to check for exposed refuse and signs of rats, mice, and insects. If conditions needed correction, they were to recommend the actions that should be taken.

The crew was driven in a department car to the first inspection site, an apartment house at 124 Grand Street, arriving at 11:30 A.M. When the crew members inspected the apartment house, they discovered rats and holes in the baseboards in several of the apartments. The landlord had not placed enough bait boxes in the basement. The Crew Chief recommended that an exterminator be scheduled to treat the building. The crew left the building at 12:05 P.M. and walked to the next inspection site at 129 Grand Street.

The crew arrived at the second site at 12:10 P.M. and left at 12:40 P.M. Because the crew found rats and roaches in the building, the Crew Chief immediately called the office and made arrangements for an exterminator to treat the building that afternoon. The Crew Chief recommended that the building should be re-inspected the following week to see if the exterminating had been successful.

The crew workers walked to the next inspection site, a vacant lot on Lucke Street, across the street from an apartment building at 350 Lucke Street. They observed that refuse covered much of the area of the vacant lot. The Crew Chief recommended that a clean-up team be scheduled to remove refuse from the lot.

The crew's last inspection of the day was a building at 300 Lucke Street. They walked to this site, arrived at 1:00 P.M., and stayed for an hour. They inspected several apartments in the building to see if a recent extermination had been successful. Upon seeing that no further work was needed at the site, they returned to their office by subway.

2 (#2)

The Crew Chief arrived at the office at 3:00 P.M. and made out the following FIELD VISIT REPORT form:

FIELD VISIT REPORT FORM

1. Date _____
2. Time Arrived at First Site _____
3. Purpose of Field Visit _____
   _____
4. Number of Persons in Crew (Not including Crew Chief (Pest Control) _____
5. Transportation _____
6. Number of Sites Visited _____
7. Addresses of Sites Visited _____
   _____
   _____
8. Conditions Noted _____
   _____
   _____
9. Recommendations _____
   _____
   _____
10. Arrangements Made by Crew Chief While in the Field _____
    _____
    _____
11. Time Left Last Site _____

1. Which of the following should be entered on line 2?   1.____
   A. 11:30 A.M.   B. 12:05 P.M.
   C. 12:10 P.M.   D. 12:40 P.M.

2. Which of the following should be entered on line 3?   2.____
   A. Exterminate apartment buildings that have rats and mice
   B. Examine various sites for exposed refuse and signs of rats, mice, and insects
   C. Inspect work done by clean-up team
   D. Clean up lots that are covered with refuse

3. The number that should be entered on line 4 is   3.____
   A. 3   B. 5   C. 8   D. 9

4. Which of the following should be entered on line 6?   4.____
   A. 3   B. 4   C. 5   D. 6

5. Each of the following should be entered on line 7 EXCEPT

   A. 124 Grand Street B. 129 Grand Street
   C. 300 Lucke Street D. 350 Lucke Street

6. Each of the following should be entered on line 8 EXCEPT the presence of

   A. holes in the baseboards at 124 Grand Street
   B. insects, rats, and mice at 300 Lucke Street
   C. refuse at the vacant lot on Lucke Street
   D. rats and roaches at 129 Grand Street

7. Which of the following should be entered on line 5?

   A. Department car to first site, subway between sites
   B. Subway to first site, walked between sites
   C. Walked to first site, department car between sites
   D. Department car to first site, walked between sites

8. All of the following should be entered on line 9 EXCEPT:

   A. Extermination at 124 Grand Street to remove rats
   B. Clean-up at the lot on Lucke Street to remove refuse
   C. Follow-up visit at 129 Grand Street to determine success of extermination
   D. Clean-up building at 300 Lucke Street to end infestation

9. Which of the following should be entered on line 10?

   A. Extermination of building at 129 Grand Street
   B. Extermination of building at 124 Grand Street
   C. Clean-up of lot on Lucke Street
   D. Clean-up of building at 300 Lucke Street

10. Which of the following should be entered on line 11?
    _____ P.M.

    A. 12:40   B. 1:00   C. 2:00   D. 3:00

KEY (CORRECT ANSWERS)

1. A
2. B
3. C
4. B
5. D

6. B
7. D
8. D
9. A
10. C

EXAMINATION SECTION
TEST 1

DIRECTIONS: Each question or incomplete statement is followed by several suggested answers or completions. Select the one that BEST answers the question or completes the statement. *PRINT THE LETTER OF THE CORRECT ANSWER IN THE SPACE AT THE RIGHT.*

Questions 1-4.

DIRECTIONS: Questions 1 through 4 are to be answered on the basis of the information provided in the paragraph below.

Rodent control must be planned carefully in order to insure its success. This means that more knowledge is needed about the habits and favorite breeding places of Domestic Rats, than any other kind. A favorite breeding place for Domestic Rats is known to be in old or badly constructed buildings. Rats find these buildings very comfortable for making nests. However, the only way to gain this kind of detailed knowledge about rats is through careful study.

1. According to the above paragraph, rats find comfortable nesting places 1.____

    A. in old buildings   B. in pipes
    C. on roofs   D. in sewers

2. The paragraph states that the BEST way to learn all about the favorite nesting places of rats is by 2.____

    A. asking people   B. careful study
    C. using traps   D. watching ratholes

3. According to the paragraph, in order to insure the success of rodent control, it is necessary to 3.____

    A. design better bait   B. give out more information
    C. plan carefully   D. use pesticides

4. The paragraph states that the MOST important rats to study are _____ rats. 4.____

    A. African   B. Asian   C. Domestic   D. European

Questions 5-8.

DIRECTIONS: Questions 5 through 8 are to be answered on the basis of the following paragraph.

A few people who live in old tenements have the bad habit of throwing garbage out of their windows, especially if there is an empty lot near their building. Sometimes the garbage is food, sometimes the garbage is half-empty soda cans. Sometimes the garbage is a little bit of both mixed together. These people just don't care about keeping the lot clean.

5. The paragraph states that throwing garbage out of windows is a   5._____

   A. bad habit   B. dangerous thing to do
   C. good thing to do   D. good way to feed rats

6. According to the paragraph, an empty lot next to an old tenement is sometimes used as   6._____
   a place to

   A. hold local gang meetings   B. play ball
   C. throw garbage   D. walk dogs

7. According to the paragraph, which of the following throw garbage out of their windows? 7._____

   A. Nobody   B. Everybody
   C. Most people   D. Some people

8. According to the paragraph, the kinds of garbage thrown out of windows are   8._____

   A. candy and cigarette butts
   B. food and half-empty soda cans
   C. fruit and vegetables
   D. rice and bread

Questions 9-12.

DIRECTIONS: Questions 9 through 12 are to be answered on the basis of the following paragraph.

The game that is recognised all over the world as an all-American game is the game of baseball. As a matter of fact, baseball heroes like Joe DiMaggio, Willie Mays, and Babe Ruth, were as famous in their day as movie stars Robert Redford, Paul Newman, and Clint Eastwood are now. All these men have had the experience of being mobbed by fans whenever they put in an appearance anywhere in the world. Such unusual popularity makes it possible for stars like these to earn at least as much money off the job as on the job. It didn't take manufacturers and advertising men long to discover that their sales of shaving lotion, for instance, increased when they got famous stars to advertise their product for them on radio and television.

9. According to the paragraph, baseball is known everywhere as a(n) _____ game.   9._____

   A. all-American   B. fast
   C. unusual   D. tough

10. According to the paragraph, being so well known means that it is possible for people like   10._____
    Willie Mays and Babe Ruth to

    A. ask for anything and get it
    B. make as much money off the job as on it
    C. travel anywhere free of charge
    D. watch any game free of charge

11. According to the paragraph, which of the following are known all over the world?   11._____

    A. Baseball heroes   B. Advertising men
    C. Manufacturers   D. Basketball heroes

12. According to the paragraph, it is possible to sell much more shaving lotion on television and radio if   12._____

    A. the commercials are in color instead of black and white
    B. you can get a prize with each bottle of shaving lotion
    C. the shaving lotion makes you smell nicer than usual
    D. the shaving lotion is advertised by famous stars

Questions 13-16.

DIRECTIONS: Questions 13 through 16 are to be answered on the basis of the following paragraph.

People are very suspicious of all strangers who knock at their door. For this reason, every pest control aide, whether man or woman, must carry an identification card at all times on the job. These cards are issued by the agency the aide works for. The aide's picture is on the card. The aide's name is typed in, and the aide's signature is written on the line below. The name, address, and telephone number of the agency issuing the card is also printed on it. Once the aide shows this ID card to prove his or her identity, the tenant's time should not be taken up with small talk. The tenant should be told briefly what pest control means. The aide should be polite and ready to answer any questions the tenant may have on the subject. Then, the aide should thank the tenant for listening and say goodbye.

13. According to the above paragraph, when she visits tenants, the one item a pest control aide must ALWAYS carry with her is a(n)   13._____

    A. badge   B. driver's license
    C. identification card   D. watch

14. According to the paragraph, a pest control aide is supposed to talk to each tenant he visits   14._____

    A. at length about the agency
    B. briefly about pest control
    C. at length about family matters
    D. briefly about social security

15. According to the paragraph, the item that does NOT appear on an ID card is the   15._____

    A. address of the agency
    B. name of the agency
    C. signature of the aide
    D. social security number of the aide

16. According to the paragraph, a pest control aide carries an identification card because he must   16._____

    A. prove to tenants who he is
    B. provide the tenants with the agency's address
    C. provide the tenant with the agency's telephone number
    D. save the tenant's time

Questions 17-20.

DIRECTIONS: Questions 17 through 20 are to be answered on the basis of the following paragraph.

Very early on a summer's morning, the nicest thing to look at is a beach, before the swimmers arrive. Usually all the litter has been picked up from the sand by the Park Department clean-up crew. Everything is quiet. All you can hear are the waves breaking, and the sea gulls calling to each other. The beach opens to the public at 10 A.M. Long before that time, however, long lines of eager men, women, and children have driven up to the entrance. They form long lines that wind around the beach waiting for the signal to move.

17. According to the paragraph, before 10 A.M., long lines are formed that are made up of

    A. cars
    B. clean-up crews
    C. men, women, and children
    D. Park Department trucks

18. The season referred to in the above paragraph is

    A. fall   B. summer   C. winter   D. spring

19. The place the paragraph is describing is a

    A. beach
    B. park
    C. golf course
    D. tennis court

20. According to the paragraph, one of the things you notice early in the morning is that

    A. radios are playing
    B. swimmers are there
    C. the sand is dirty
    D. the litter is gone

Questions 21-30.

DIRECTIONS: In Questions 21 through 30, select the answer which means MOST NEARLY the SAME as the capitalized word in the sentence.

21. He received a large REWARD.
    In this sentence, the word REWARD means

    A. capture
    B. recompense
    C. key
    D. praise

22. The aide was asked to TRANSMIT a message. In this sentence, the word TRANSMIT means

    A. change   B. send   C. take   D. type

23. The pest control aide REQUESTED the tenant to call the Health Department.
    In this sentence, the word REQUESTED means the pest control aide

    A. asked   B. helped   C. informed   D. warned

24. The driver had to RETURN the Health Department's truck. In this sentence, the word RETURN means

    A. borrow   B. fix   C. give back   D. load up

25. The aide discussed the PURPOSE of the visit. In this sentence, the word PURPOSE means

    A. date B. hour C. need D. reason.

26. The tenant SUSPECTED the aide who knocked at her door. In this sentence, the word SUSPECTED means

    A. answered
    B. called
    C. distrusted
    D. welcomed

27. The aide was POSITIVE that the child hit her. In this sentence, the word POSITIVE means

    A. annoyed B. certain C. sorry D. surprised

28. The tenant DECLINED to call the Health Department. In this sentence, the word DECLINED means

    A. agreed B. decided C. refused D. wanted

29. The aide ARRIVED on time.
    In this sentence, the word ARRIVED means

    A. awoke B. came C. left D. delayed

30. The salesman had to DELIVER books to each person he visited.
    In this sentence, the word DELIVER means

    A. give B. lend C. mail D. sell

KEY (CORRECT ANSWERS)

1. A	11. A	21. B
2. B	12. D	22. B
3. C	13. C	23. A
4. C	14. B	24. C
5. A	15. D	25. D
6. C	16. A	26. C
7. D	17. C	27. B
8. B	18. B	28. C
9. A	19. A	29. B
10. B	20. D	30. A

TEST 2

DIRECTIONS: Each question or incomplete statement is followed by several suggested answers or completions. Select the one that BEST answers the question or completes the statement. *PRINT THE LETTER OF THE CORRECT ANSWER IN THE SPACE AT THE RIGHT.*

Questions 1-10.

DIRECTIONS: In Questions 1 through 10, pick the word that means MOST NEARLY the OPPOSITE of the capitalize word in the sentence.

1. It is possible to CONSTRUCT a rat-proof home. The opposite of CONSTRUCT is   1.____
   A. build   B. erect   C. plant   D. wreck

2. The pest control aide had to REPAIR the flat tire. The opposite of the word REPAIR is   2.____
   A. destroy   B. fix   C. mend   D. patch

3. The pest control aide tried to SHOUT the answer. The opposite of the word SHOUT is   3.____
   A. scream   B. shriek   C. whisper   D. yell

4. Daily VISITS are the best.   4.____
   The opposite of the word VISITS is
   A. absences   B. exercises   C. lessons   D. trials

5. It is important to ARRIVE early in the morning. The opposite of the word ARRIVE is   5.____
   A. climb   B. descend   C. enter   D. leave

6. Jorge is a group LEADER.   6.____
   The opposite of the word LEADER is
   A. boss   B. chief   C. follower   D. overseer

7. The EXTERIOR of the house needs painting.   7.____
   The opposite of the word EXTERIOR is
   A. inside   B. outdoors   C. outside   D. surface

8. He CONCEDED the victory.   8.____
   The opposite of the word CONCEDED is
   A. admitted   B. denied   C. granted   D. reported

9. He watched the team BEGIN.   9.____
   The opposite of the word BEGIN is
   A. end   B. fail   C. gather   D. win

10. Your handwriting is ILLEGIBLE.   10.____
    The opposite of the word ILLEGIBLE is
    A. clear   B. confused   C. jumbled   D. unclear

Questions 11-15.

DIRECTIONS: Questions 11 through 15 are to be answered by following the instructions given in each question. Note that 5 possible answers have been given for these questions ONLY. Therefore, for these questions, your choice may be A, B, C, D, or E.

11. Add:
    $12\frac{1}{2}$
    $2\frac{1}{4}$
    $3\frac{1}{4}$

    The CORRECT answer is

    A. 17   B. 174   C. 174   D. 17 3/4   E. 18

12. Subtract: 150
              -80

    The CORRECT answer is

    A. 70   B. 80   C. 130   D. 150   E. 230

13. After cleaning up some lots in the East Bronx, five cleanup crews loaded the following amounts of garbage on trucks:
    Crew No. 1 loaded 2 1/4 tons
    Crew No. 2 loaded 3 tons
    Crew No. 3 loaded 1 1/4 tons
    Crew No. 4 loaded 2 1/4 tons
    Crew No. 5 loaded 1/2 ton
    The TOTAL number of tons of garbage loaded was

    A. 8   B. 8 1/4   C. 8 3/4   D. 9   E. 9 1/4

14. Subtract: 17 3/4
              - 7 1/4

    The CORRECT answer is

    A. 7 1/2   B. 10 1/2   C. 14 1/4   D. 17 3/4   E. 25

15. Yesterday, Tom and Bill each received 10 leaflets about rat control. Each supermarket in the neighborhood was supposed to receive one of these leaflets. When the day was over, Tom had 8 leaflets left. Bill had no leaflets left. How many supermarkets got leaflets yesterday?

    A. 8   B. 10   C. 12   D. 18   E. 20

Questions 16-20.

DIRECTIONS: Questions 16 through 20 are to be answered ONLY on the basis of the information in the following statement and chart, DAILY WORK REPORT FORM (Chart A).

Assume that you are a member of the Pest Control Truck Crew Number 1. Julio Rivera is your Crew Chief. The crew is supposed to report to work at nine o'clock in the morning, Since you are the first to show up, at ten minutes before nine, on 5/24 Rivera asks you to help him out by filling in the Daily Work Report Form for him. Driver Hal Williams shows up at nine, and Driver Rick Smith shows up ten minutes after Williams.

DAILY WORK REPORT FORM (Chart A)

Block #1 Crew No.	Block #2 Date	
Block #3 TRUCKS IN USE Truck # _____ # _____ # _____ # _____ # _____ # _____ # _____ # _____ # _____ # _____	Block #4 DRIVER'S NAME _____ _____ _____ _____ _____ _____ _____ _____ _____	Block #5 TIME OF ARRIVAL A.M. P.M.
Block #6 TRUCKS OUT OF ORDER # _____ # _____ # _____ # _____ #	Block #7 ADDRESS OF CLEAN-UP SITE No._____ Street_____	Block #8 Borough Block #9 Signature of Crew Chief

16. According to the above statement, the entry that belongs in Block #9 is   16.____

    A. Julio Rivera   B. June Stevens
    C. Jim Watson   D. Hal Williams

17. According to the above statement, the entry that should be made in Block #2 is   17.____

    A. 9:00 A.M.   B. 9:10 P.M.   C. 5/24   D. 7/24

18. The names of Hal Williams and Rick Smith should appear in Block #   18.____

    A. 4   B. 6   C. 7   D. 9

19. Rick Smith's time of arrival should be entered in Block #5 as _____ A.M.

    A. 8:50   B. 8:55   C. 9:00   D. 9:10

20. According to the statement, the entry that should be made in Block #1 is

    A. zero   B. one   C. 5/24   D. 6/24

Questions 21-23.

DIRECTIONS: Questions 21 through 23 are to be answered on the basis of the statement shown below. Use DAILY WORK REPORT FORM (Chart A) on Page 3 as a guide.

Pete Marberg showed up at a quarter after nine, in the morning, but his truck, No. 22632441, was in the garage for repairs. Steve Marino showed up a half hour after Pete. He was assigned truck No. 6342003, which was in working order.

21. According to the above statement, truck No. 22632441 should be entered in Block #

    A. 3   B. 4   C. 6   D. 8

22. According to the above statement, Steve Marino showed up at

    A. 9:00 A.M.   B. 9:15 A.M.   C. 9:30 P.M.   D. 9:45 A.M.

23. According to the above statement, Steve Marino's truck number belongs in Block #3. The number entered there should be

    A. 22632441   B. 6342003   C. 6432003   D. 26232441

Questions 24-30.

DIRECTIONS: Questions 24 through 30 are to be answered ONLY on basis of the information in the statements above ea question and the following chart, DAILY GARBAGE COLLECTION REPORT (Chart B).

DAILY GARBAGE COLLECTION REPORT (Chart B)				
Block #1	Block #2	Block #3	Block #4	Block #5
No. of Trucks Used For Collection	Address of Garbage Pick-Up	Amount of Garbage Collected	Amount of Garbage Unloaded	Hours During Which Garbage Was Unloaded
#456	45 Southwest	1/2 ton	1/2 ton	From 7 AM To 8 AM
TOTALS _____		Block #6 Total Amount of Garbage Collected By All Trucks	Block #7 Total Amount of Garbage Unloaded By All Trucks	Block #8 Total Amount of Time Spent Unloading Of All Trucks

24. Truck # 2437752 started unloading garbage at ten o'clock Monday morning and finished unloading its garbage that afternoon. The clock looked like this when the job was done.
    The time entries that should be recorded in Block #5 are
    A. 10 A.M. and 12:15 P.M.
    B. 10 P.M. and 12:30 A.M.
    C. 10 P.M. and 12:00 A.M.
    D. 10 A.M. and 3:00 P.M.

25. Truck # 8967432 had to pick up a load of garbage from 911 South Avenue. It took the crew until 11:00 A.M. to load the garbage.
    According to this statement, the item 911 South Avenue should be entered in Block #

    A. 1   B. 2   C. 3   D. 4

26. On Tuesday, truck # 124356 unloaded 4 ton of garbage, truck # 2437752 unloaded J ton of garbage, and truck # 435126 unloaded 1/2 ton of garbage.
    The TOTAL amount of garbage unloaded by the three trucks on Tuesday should be entered in Block #

    A. 3   B. 4   C. 5   D. 8

27. On Wednesday, it took truck # 4050607 from 2 P.M. to 6 P.M. to unload 1 ton of garbage. It took truck # 7040650 from 1 P.M. to 2 P.M. to unload 1/4 ton of garbage. These were the only trucks working that day.
    The TOTAL amount of time it took for both trucks to unload garbage was _____ hours.

    A. 5   B. 6   C. 7   D. 8

28. The amount of garbage collected by one truck should be entered in the DAILY GARBAGE COLLECTION REPORT FORM in Block #

    A. 3   B. 6   C. 7   D. 8

29. Truck # 557799010 reported to 1020 Hudson River Alley to pick up garbage from an empty lot.
    This information should be entered in the DAILY GARBAGE COLLECTION REPORT FORM in Block # _____ and Block # _____ .

    A. 1; 4   B. 2; 5   C. 1; 2   D. 2; 3

30. It took the Pest Control Truck crew from 8 in the morning to 12 noon to unload the garbage it collected the night before.
    This information should be entered in the DAILY GARBAGE COLLECTION REPORT FORM under Block #

    A. 4   B. 5   C. 6   D. 7

KEY (CORRECT ANSWERS)

1. D	11. E	21. C
2. A	12. A	22. D
3. C	13. E	23. B
4. A	14. B	24. D
5. D	15. C	25. B
6. C	16. A	26. B
7. A	17. C	27. A
8. B	18. A	28. A
9. A	19. D	29. C
10. A	20. B	30. B

EXAMINATION SECTION
TEST 1

DIRECTIONS: Each question or incomplete statement is followed by several suggested answers or completions. Select the one that BEST answers the question or completes the statement. *PRINT THE LETTER OF THE CORRECT ANSWER IN THE SPACE AT THE RIGHT.*

1. In his dealings with tenants, an exterminator will find that tenants will usually cooperate willingly to carry out a legitimate request if they

    A. are asked to do it at the time the exterminator leaves
    B. have lived in the building for more than a year
    C. fear the exterminator's official authority
    D. understand the reason for the request

1.____

2. When planning his work schedule at a housing project, an exterminator should FIRST determine

    A. how the work should be done
    B. what work has to be done
    C. when the work must be completed
    D. what equipment and supplies are needed

2.____

3. Assume that your foreman and you disagree as to how a certain bait should be applied. You think your way is better.
Under these circumstances, you should generally

    A. be frank and tell your foreman why you think your way is better
    B. discuss the matter with a higher ranking member of the pest control section
    C. ignore what the foreman says and do it your way
    D. postpone further discussion until your foreman is in a better mood

3.____

4. Your foreman reprimands you for creating a safety hazard by not closing containers of pesticides when they are not in use. However, you know that you closed the containers after you had finished using them. These containers were left open by another exterminator.
It would be MOST advisable for you to close the containers and take which one of the following actions?

    A. Find out who the exterminator was and get this person to tell the foreman what really happened
    B. Complain to other exterminators about your foreman's lack of fairness and judgment
    C. Notify your foreman's boss of the unjust accusation
    D. Tell the foreman that the containers were left open by another exterminator

4.____

5. Of the following, the MOST advisable thing for you to do if your foreman asks you to operate a piece of equipment you do not know how to handle is to

    A. ask one of the other exterminators if he could do the job for you this time
    B. ask one of the men in the maintenance department of the housing development to show you how to use it

5.____

27

C. tell your foreman that you do not know how to operate it
D. try it out until you figure out how it works

6. Suppose that you receive a shipment of 50 rat snap-traps from a hardware dealer. When you unpack them, you find that in seven of the traps, the springs and triggers are not fastened securely to the trap because there are deep cracks in the wood where they are attached.
Of the following, it would be MOST advisable for you to

A. cover the cracks with masking tape and put all the traps on the stock shelf in the shop
B. list only 43 traps in your stock records and put the damaged traps aside for salvage
C. send all the traps back to the hardware dealer
D. tell your foreman about the damaged traps

7. Of the following, the MAIN purpose of a safety training program is to

A. fix the blame for accidents
B. describe accidents which have occurred
C. hold the Housing Exterminators responsible for unsafe working conditions
D. make the Housing Exterminators aware of the basic causes of accidents

8. When administering first aid to a person suffering from shock as a result of an accident, of the following, it is MOST important to

A. cover the person and keep him warm
B. apply artificial respiration
C. prop him up in a sitting position
D. massage the person in order to aid blood circulation

9. Assume you have just been appointed. You notice that certain equipment which is assigned to you is defective and that use of this equipment may eventually result in unnecessary costs and perhaps injury to you.
The BEST thing for you to do is to

A. speak to the maintenance men in the project about repairing the equipment
B. discuss the matter with your foreman
C. mind your own business since you have just been appointed
D. speak to other exterminators and find out if they had any experience with defective equipment

10. Assume you are working in a project building and one of the housing caretakers has just been seriously injured in an accident in the slop sink room.
Your FIRST concern should be to

A. help the injured man
B. find the cause of the accident
C. report the accident to your foreman
D. report the accident to the caretaker's boss

11. Assume a mass of extension cords plugged into one outlet in a pest control shop results in overloading the electrical circuit and causes a fire.
    Which of the following types of extinguisher should be used to put out the fire?

    A. Carbon dioxide (CO_2)
    B. Water
    C. Soda acid
    D. Carbon tetrachloride

12. Manufacturers of chemical pesticides usually recommend that special precautions be taken when the chemicals are used.
    Of the following, which one would a manufacturer be LEAST likely to recommend?

    A. Wear leather gloves
    B. Wear a respirator
    C. Wear safety goggles
    D. Have a first aid kit available

Questions 13-15.

DIRECTIONS: Questions 13 through 15 consist of groups of statements that have to do with safety precautions and procedures. Choose the statement in each group that is NOT correct.

13. A. The label on the original container of the pesticide should be read before each use.
    B. Pest control equipment should be cleaned regularly.
    C. Whenever there is a choice of chemicals, the chemical which is less hazardous to humans should be used at all times.
    D. For the transfer of concentrates from drums, either threaded taps or drum pumps should be used.

14. A. Do not use a petroleum base on an asphalt tile floor.
    B. Do not spray oil base sprays on material colored with oil soluble dyes.
    C. Do not use respirators.
    D. Do not use pesticides which are highly poisonous to mammals.

15. The following statements deal with disposal of empty gallon metal containers which held highly toxic organic phosphate insecticides.

    A. Do not reuse these containers.
    B. Pour one pint of water into the empty container, add bicarbonate of soda, and bury the container of rinse solution at least 18 inches below ground.
    C. Wet all inner surfaces with the proper rinse solution.
    D. Punch holes in the top and bottom of the can, crush the can and bury deeply in an isolated location.

KEY (CORRECT ANSWERS)

1. D
2. B
3. A
4. D
5. C

6. D
7. D
8. A
9. B
10. A

11. A
12. A
13. C
14. C
15. B

———

TEST 2

DIRECTIONS: Each question or incomplete statement is followed by several suggested answers or completions. Select the one that BEST answers the question or completes the statement. *PRINT THE LETTER OF THE CORRECT ANSWER IN THE SPACE AT THE RIGHT.*

1. There are 22 boxes of rat mix in a certain pest control shop.
   If each box contains 7 1/2 pounds of rat mix, the TOTAL amount of rat mix in the shop is _____ pounds.

   A. 165   B. 172 1/2   C. 180   D. 182 1/2

   1._____

2. A pest control shop has a supply of 26 one-gallon cans of insecticide.
   If the exterminator works 5 days a week and uses 32 ounces of the liquid a day, the number of work-weeks this supply of insecticide will last is MOST NEARLY

   A. 10   B. 20   C. 28   D. 32

   2._____

3. A certain supplier packs two dozen mouse traps to a box. If the exterminator gets a delivery of 20 boxes and finds that two of these boxes are half-full, the TOTAL number of traps the exterminator received from this supplier is

   A. 408   B. 432   C. 456   D. 480

   3._____

4. Assume that a truck which contains a shipment of pesticides ia parked outside your exterminating shop. You are able to unload the truck in one hour.
   How long would it take four exterminators, starting at the same time and working at the same rate as you, to unload four trucks similar to the one you unloaded?

   A. 15 minutes   B. 1 hour
   C. 2 hours   D. 4 hours

   4._____

5. A certain building in a housing development has 142 apartments. It takes on exterminator an average of six minutes to treat one apartment.
   At that rate, approximately how long should it take him to treat ALL 142 apartments? _____ hours.

   A. 2   B. 14   C. 24   D. 85

   5._____

6. A crate contains 3 pieces of pesticide equipment weighing 73, 84, and 47 pounds, respectively.
   If the crate is lifted by 4 exterminators, each lifting one corner of the crate, the average number of pounds, in addition to the weight of the crate, lifted by each of the exterminators is

   A. 51   B. 65   C. 71   D. 78

   6._____

7. A stack of cartons containing pesticides is 10 cartons long, 9 cartons wide, and 5 cartons high.
   The number of cartons in the stack is

   A. 24   B. 55   C. 95   D. 450

   7._____

8. Assume that you have bags of corn meal, each of the same weight. The total weight of 25 bags is 125 pounds.
   How many of these bags would it take to make a TOTAL weight of 50 pounds?

   A. 2 B. 5 C. 6 D. 10

9. You are working in the sub-basement of a project building and the foreman tells you to get two boards from the maintenance shop to stand on. One of the boards is 5 yards long and the other is 3 1/2 feet long.
   The TOTAL length, in feet, of the two boards is

   A. 8 1/2 B. 9 1/2 C. 17 1/2 D. 18 1/2

10. Three hundred plastic bags of rat mix, each bag weighing four ounces, are packed in a carton. The carton weighed one pound before the rat mix was packed in it.
    The TOTAL weight of the filled carton is _____ pounds.

    A. 37 1/2 B. 38 1/2 C. 75 D. 76

11. In a certain project, an exterminator is told to spray 120 apartments, 40 apartments, 20 basements, 80 apartments, 50 storerooms, and 10 compactors.
    The TOTAL number of apartments which should be sprayed is

    A. 240 B. 260 C. 310 D. 320

Questions 12-15.

DIRECTIONS: Questions 12 through 15 are to be answered SOLELY on the basis of the following information.

The insects you, as a housing exterminators will control are just a minute fraction of the millions which inhabit the world. Man does well to hold his own in the face of the constant pressures that insects continue to exert upon him. Not only are the total numbers tremendous, but the number of individual kinds, or species, certainly exceeds 800,000 — a number greater than that of all other animals combined. Many of these are beneficial but some are especially competitive with man. Not only are insects numerous, but they are among the most adaptable of all animals. In their many forms, they are fitted for almost any specific way of life. Their adaptability, combined with their tremendous rate of reproduction, gives insects an unequaled potential for survival!

The food of insects includes almost anything that can be eaten by any other animal as well as many things which cannot even be digested by any other animals. Most insects do not harm the products of man or carry diseases harmful to him; however, many do carry diseases and others feed on his food and manufactured goods. Some are adapted to living only in open areas while others are able to live in extremely confined spaces. All of these factors combined, make the insects a group of animals having many members which are a nuisance to man and thus of great importance to the housing exterminator.

The control of insects requires an understanding of their way of life. Thus, it is necessary for the housing exterminator to understand the anatomy of the insect, its method of growth, the time it takes for the insect to grow from egg to adult, its habits, the stage of its life history in which it causes damage, its food, and its common living places. In order to obtain the best *control, it is especially important to be able to identify correctly the specific insect involved because without this knowledge, it is impossible to prescribe a proper treatment.*

12. Which one of the following is a CORRECT statement about the insect population of the world, according to the above paragraph?
The

   A. total number of insects is less than the total number of all other animals combined
   B. number of species of insects is greater than the number of species of all other animals combined
   C. total number of harmful insects is greater than the total number of those which are not harmful
   D. number of species of harmless insects is less than the number of species of those which are harmful

13. Insects will be controlled MOST efficiently if the housing exterminator

   A. understands why the insects are so numerous
   B. knows what insects he is dealing with
   C. sees if the insects compete with man
   D. is able to identify the food which the insects digest

14. According to the above passage, insects are of importance to an exterminator PRIMARILY because they

   A. can be annoying, destructive, and harmful to man
   B. are able to thrive in very small spaces
   C. cause damage during their growth stages
   D. are so adaptable that they can adjust to any environment

15. According to the above passage, insects can eat

   A. everything that any other living thing can eat
   B. man's food and things which he makes
   C. anything which other animals can't digest
   D. only food and food products

KEY (CORRECT ANSWERS)

1.	A	6.	A
2.	B	7.	D
3.	C	8.	D
4.	B	9.	D
5.	B	10.	D

11.	A
12.	B
13.	B
14.	A
15.	B

EXAMINATION SECTION
TEST 1

DIRECTIONS: Each question or incomplete statement is followed by several suggested answers or completions. Select the one that BEST answers the question or completes the statement. *PRINT THE LETTER OF THE CORRECT ANSWER IN THE SPACE AT THE RIGHT.*

1. Suppose you have 15 5/6 ounces of a certain chemical on hand.
   If you later receive shipments of 6 1/2 ounces and 8 3/4 ounces of this chemical, the TOTAL number of ounces you should then have on hand is

   A. 29 7/8 B. 30 5/6 C. 31 1/2 D. 31 3/4

2. You are told to prepare 60 pounds of 2% pyrethrum dust using talc and 5% pyrethrum dust concentrate.
   What is the amount of concentrate that is required in the mixture?
   _____ pounds.

   A. 24 B. 28 C. 30 1/2 D. 36

3. In the pest control shop of a certain housing development, there is a supply of 4 one-gallon containers of insecticide. This week, the exterminator will use up five quarts of this insecticide in his work, and for each week thereafter he will use up five quarts. Deliveries are made on the first day of the week.
   Next week, and each week thereafter, the shop will get a delivery of one gallon of insecticide.
   The exterminator will need an additional supply of insecticide by the end of the _____ week.

   A. 4th B. 12th C. 24th D. 29th

Questions 4-7.

DIRECTIONS: Questions 4 through 7 are to be answered SOLELY on the basis of the following passage.

   Sometimes an exterminator has to use a crowbar, for example, to open wooden crates that contain supplies which are shipped to the exterminating shop. He should know how to handle a crowbar so that he can use it safely. The danger involved in using a crowbar is that it may slip. A dull, broken crowbar is more likely to slip than one which has a sharp edge and a good "bite." If the crowbar should slip or the object being opened should move suddenly, an exterminator's hand might be pinched or he might fall. The way in which he holds the crowbar and how he stands when using it can prevent such accidents. His hands should be dry when he uses a crowbar and, if he is wearing gloves, they should be free from grease. He should not work with the crowbar between his legs. When they are not being used, crowbars should be kept in a rack in the exterminating shop where they can not fall on someone or cause anyone to trip.

4. Of the following, the BEST title for the above passage is

   A. Proper Position When Using a Crowbar
   B. Tools Used by Exterminators

C. Using a Crowbar Safely
D. When to Use a Crowbar

5. A crowbar is MOST likely to slip if it

   A. has a good *bite*
   B. has a sharp edge
   C. is dull and broken
   D. is handled without gloves

6. Crowbars should be stored in a rack when they are not being used so that they will

   A. be easy to get at
   B. not cause accidents
   C. not be broken
   D. not be stolen

7. A worker should NOT use a crowbar if

   A. he is wearing gloves
   B. his hands are wet
   C. it has not been kept in a rack
   D. it has a sharp edge

Questions 8-12.

DIRECTIONS: Questions 8 through 12 are to be answered SOLELY on the basis of the following passage.

Lots of exterminators still think accidents just happen - that they are due to bad luck. Nothing could be further from the truth. Evidence of this is in the drop in accidents among employees of the City of New York since the Safety Program started. The one-out-of-a-hundred accidents that cannot be prevented might be called "Acts of God." They are things like lightning, earthquakes, tornadoes, and tidal waves that we are powerless to prevent - although we can take precautions against them which will cut down the accident rate. The other ninety-nine percent of the accidents clearly have a manmade cause. If you trace back far enough, you'll find that somewhere, somehow, someone could have done something to prevent these accidents. For just about every accident, there is some fellow who fouled up. He didn't protect himself, he didn't use the right equipment, he wasn't alert, he lost his temper, he didn't have his mind on his work, he was "kidding around," or he took a shortcut because he was just too lazy. We must all work together to improve safety and prevent injury and death.

8. The one of the following titles which BEST describes the subject matter of the above passage is

   A. Acts of God
   B. The Importance of Safety Consciousness
   C. Safety in New York City
   D. Working Together

9. After New York City began to operate a safety program, it was found that

   A. the number of accidents were reduced
   B. production decreased
   C. accidents stayed the same but employees were more careful
   D. the element of bad luck did not change

10. One cause of accidents that is NOT mentioned in the above passage is

    A. failure to keep alert
    B. taking a shortcut
    C. using the wrong equipment
    D. working too fast

11. The number of accidents caused by such things as hurricanes can be

    A. changed only by an *Act of God*
    B. eliminated by strict adherence to safety rules
    C. increased by being too careful
    D. reduced by proper safety precautions

12. The percentage of accidents that occur as a result of things that CANNOT be prevented is approximately _____ percent.

    A. 1   B. 10   C. 50   D. 99

Questions 13-15.

DIRECTIONS: Questions 13 through 15 are to be answered SOLELY on the basis of the following passage.

An exterminator should call the Fire Department for any fire except a small one in a wastebasket. This kind of fire can be put out with a fire extinguisher. If the exterminator is not sure about the size of the fire, he should not wait to find out how big it is. He should call the Fire Department at once.

Every exterminator should know what to do when a fire starts. He should know, how to use the firefighting tools in the building and how to call the Fire Department. He should also know where the nearest fire alarm box is. But the most important thing for an exterminator to do in case of fire is to avoid panic.

13. If there is a small fire in a wastebasket, an exterminator should

    A. call the Fire Department
    B. let it burn itself out
    C. open a window
    D. put it out with a fire extinguisher

14. In case of fire, the MOST important thing for an exterminator to do is to

    A. find out how big it is
    B. keep calm
    C. leave the building right away
    D. report to his boss

15. If a large fire starts while he is at work, an exterminator should always FIRST
    A. call the Fire Department
    B. notify the Housing Superintendent
    C. remove inflammables from the building
    D. use a fire extinguisher

KEY (CORRECT ANSWERS)

1. C
2. A
3. B
4. C
5. C

6. B
7. B
8. B
9. A
10. D

11. D
12. A
13. D
14. B
15. A

TEST 2

DIRECTIONS: Each question or incomplete statement is followed by several suggested answers or completions. Select the one that BEST answers the question or completes the statement. *PRINT THE LETTER OF THE CORRECT ANSWER IN THE SPACE AT THE RIGHT.*

1. If a space treatment device covers 1,000 cubic feet in six seconds, how long should it run in order to treat a room that is 30 feet long, 20 feet wide, and 15 feet high? 1.____

   A. 18 seconds
   B. 54 seconds
   C. 1 minute 24 seconds
   D. 1 minute 48 seconds

2. If you have to prepare five gallons of 0.5 Diazinon emulsion using water and 20% Diazinon emulsifiable concentrate, what is the amount of concentrate that is necessary? 2.____
   _____ ounces

   A. 1.6   B. 3.2   C. 16.0   D. 64.0

Questions 3-12.

DIRECTIONS: Questions 3 through 12 are to be answered SOLELY on the basis of the following instructions.

INSTRUCTIONS FOR PREPARATION AND PLACEMENT OF RAT BAITS

1. *Fresh baits are the most acceptable to rats, so mix only enough bait for current needs. Use a binder of molasses or of vegetable, mineral or fish oil in cereal or dry baits to hold the poison and the dry bait together and to aid in mixing.*
2. *Mix an emetic, usually tartar emetic, with zinc phosphide and other more toxic bait formulations to protect animals other than rodents, even though acceptability of such baits to the rodents is thereby reduced.*
3. *Mix bait as directed. Too much poison may give the bait a strong taste or odor. Too little will not kill buy may result in "bait shyness." Excessive amounts of poison increase the danger to man and to domestic animals.*
4. *Mix baits well. Poor mixing results in non-uniform baits and poor kills and speeds development of bait shyness. Mechanical bait-mixing equipment is necessary where large quantities of bait are mixed routinely.*
5. *Clearly label poisons and mixing equipment. Do not use bait-mixing equipment for other purposes. Lock up poisons and mixing equipment when not in use. Treat all poisons with respect. Read and follow all label instructions. Avoid inhaling powders or getting poisons on hands, clothes or utensils from which they may reach the mouth. Wear rubber gloves when handling poisons. Always mix poisons in a well-ventilated place, particularly when mixing dry ingredients.*
6. *If anticoagulant baits are used, they should be placed in paper, metal, or plastic pie plates or in permanent bait stations. Be liberal in baiting. For anticoagulants to be fully effective, repeated doses must be consumed by every rodent at a given location for a period of five or more consecutive days.*
7. *Protect animals other than domestic rodents, and shield baits from the weather under shelter or with bait boxes, boards, pipes, or cans.*

8. Note locations of all bait containers so that inspections can be made rapidly and the bait that has been consumed can be quickly replaced. (Bait consumption is generally heavy right after initial placement, making daily inspection and replacement advisable for the first S days after regular feeding begins.)
9. At each inspection, smooth the surface of the baits so that new signs of feeding will show readily. Replace moldy, wet, caked, or insect-infested baits with fresh ones. If a bait remains undisturbed for several successive inspections, move it to an area showing fresh rodent signs.
10. Use shallow bait containers fastened to the floor, or containers of sufficient weight to prevent the rodents from overturning them or dragging them to their burrows. A roofing tack driven through metal or fiber containers into the floor reduces spillage.
11. When single-dose poisons are used, wrap one-shot poison food baits in 4" x 4" paper squares to form "torpedoes" about the size of a large olive. These may be tossed readily into otherwise inaccessible places. If several types of bait such as meat, fish or cereal are to be distributed at the same time, a different color of paper should be used for each of the various types of bait.
12. Be generous with baits. Too few baits, or poorly placed baits, may miss many rodents. Bait liberally where signs of rat activity are numerous and recent. In light or moderate infestations, torpedoes containing a single-dose poison, such as red squill, have given good control when applied at a minimum rate of 20 baits per private residence. As many as 100 to 200 baits may be required for premises with heavy rodent infestations.
13. Place baits in hidden sites out of reach of children and pets.
14. Inspect and rebait as needed, using another poison and another bait material when the rats become shy of the original baits.

3. According to the above instructions, if you find, upon inspection, that your baits are overrun with insects, you should

   A. replace the baits with fresh baits
   B. move the baits to another station
   C. add more rodenticide to the baits and re-mix them
   D. apply the appropriate insecticide to the baits

4. According to the above instructions, if an exterminator wants to make sure he does NOT get poor kills, he should

   A. mix large quantities of baits routinely
   B. stick to one poison
   C. mix the baits well
   D. use deep bait containers that cannot be easily overturned

5. According to the above instructions, the equipment which is used for mixing bait should be

   A. cleaned routinely
   B. mechanically easy to handle
   C. easily disposable
   D. labeled clearly

6. According to the above instructions, making the surface of the bait smooth every time that you inspect the bait containers is

    A. *proper* because it disturbs the insect infestation of the bait
    B. *improper* because it will make the bait even less uniform if it was already mixed poorly
    C. *proper* because it will help you determine if new signs of feeding are present
    D. *improper* because it increases the presence of human odor on the bait and discourages rodents

6.____

7. According to the above instructions, if you are making a bait with zinc phosphide, it is MOST important to

    A. prepare a generous amount so you can bait liberally where signs of rat activity are numerous
    B. use molasses to insure that the bait will be uniform
    C. shield the bait from the weather
    D. mix an emetic with the bait

7.____

8. According to the above instructions, you should substitute one poison for another poison when the

    A. bait consumption is heavy after initial placement
    B. rodents become shy of the original baits
    C. poison is dangerous to domestic animals
    D. rodents are able to drag the baits to their burrows

8.____

9. According to the above instructions, when you handle poisons, you should

    A. use mechanical bait-making equipment
    B. wear rubber gloves
    C. never place them in paper plates
    D. always mix them with moist ingredients

9.____

10. According to the above instructions, if you plan to distribute several types of bait at the same time in the form of *torpedoes,* you should

    A. select only anticoagulant baits for this purpose
    B. reduce the possibility of bait spillage by driving a roofing tack through the container into the floor
    C. use a different color of paper for each of the various types of bait
    D. make sure that the rodent does not consume repeated doses for more than a period of five consecutive days at the same location

10.____

11. According to the above instructions, mixing too much poison in the bait

    A. may bring about bait shyness
    B. permits the exterminator to make less frequent reinspections
    C. increases the danger to other life
    D. may be necessary when anticoagulants are used

11.____

12. According to the above instructions, if grain is to be used as bait, 12.____
    A. rodents will not accept it if it is mixed with fish oil
    B. the exterminator will only be able to make *torpedoes*
    C. it will not be necessary to check the bait for fresh rodent signs
    D. a binder should also be used to aid in mixing

Questions 13-15.

DIRECTIONS: Questions 13 through 15 are to be answered on the basis of the information which appears in the passage below.

The German roach is the most common roach in houses in the United States. Adults are pale brown and about 1/2-inch long; both sexes have wings as long as the body, and can be distinguished from other roaches by the two dark stripes on the pronotum. The female carries its egg capsule protruding from her abdomen until the eggs are ready to hatch. This is the only common house-infesting species which carries the egg capsule for such an extended period of time. A female will usually produce 4 to 8 capsules in her lifetime. Each capsule contains 30 to 48 eggs which hatch out in about 28 days at ordinary room temperature. The completion of the nymphal stage under room conditions requires 40 to 125 days. German roaches may live as adults for as long as 303 days.

It is stated above that the German cockroach is the most commonly encountered of the house-infesting species in the United States. The reasons for this are somewhat complex, but the understanding of some of the factors involved are basic to the practice of pest control. In the first place, the German cockroach has a larger number of eggs per capsule and a shorter hatching time than do the other species. It also requires a shorter period from hatching until sexual maturity, so that within a given period of time a population of German roaches will produce a larger number of eggs. On the basis of this fact, we can state that this species has a high reproductive potential. Since the female carries the egg capsule during nearly the entire time that the embryos are developing within the egg, many hazards of the environment which may affect the eggs are avoided. This means that more nymphs are likely to hatch and that a larger portion of the reproductive potential is realized. The nymphs which hatch from each egg capsule tend to stay close to each other, and since they are often close to the female at time of hatching, there is a tendency for the population density to be high locally. Being smaller than most of the other roaches, they are able to conceal themselves in many places which are inaccessible to individuals of the larger species. All of these factors combined help to give the German cockroach an advantage with regard to group survival.

13. According to the above passage, the MOST important feature of the German roach which gives it an advantage over other roaches is its 13.____
    A. distinctive markings
    B. immunity to disease
    C. long life span
    D. power to reproduce

14. An IMPORTANT difference between an adult female German roach and an adult female of other species is the 14.____
    A. black bars or stripes which appear on the abdomen of the German roach
    B. German roach's preference for warm, moist places in which to breed

C. long period of time during which the German roach carries the egg capsule
D. presence of longer wings on the female German roach

15. A storeroom in a certain housing project has an infestation of German roaches, which includes 125 adult females. If the infestation is not treated and ordinary room temperature is maintained in the storeroom, how many eggs will hatch out during the lifetime of these females if they each lay 8 capsules containing 48 eggs each? 15.____

   A. 1,500   B. 48,000   C. 96,000   D. 303,000

KEY (CORRECT ANSWERS)

1. B
2. C
3. A
4. C
5. D

6. C
7. D
8. B
9. B
10. C

11. C
12. D
13. D
14. C
15. B

EXAMINATION SECTION

TEST 1

DIRECTIONS: Read the statements and descriptions listed in the column to the left and match each with the correct term or phrase from the list to the right. *PRINT THE LETTER OF THE CORRECT ANSWER IN THE SPACE AT THE RIGHT.*

Questions 1-10

1. Maximum amount of pesticide which can legally remain on or in any food or feed crop at harvest or animal at slaughter

2. Recognition by certifying agency that a person is competent and thus authorized to use or supervise the use of restricted-use pesticides

3. Not protected or shielded; contact with pesticide through ingestion, inhalation or skin contact

4. Risk of danger; chance that injury or harm will come to the applicator, other persons, plants or animals

5. A certified applicator who uses or supervises the use of any pesticide classified for restricted use for the purpose of producing any agricultural commodity on the property owned or rented by him or his employer or on the property of another person producing any agricultural commodity in exchange of personal services

6. Chemical or other substance that will prevent, repel, destroy or control a pest or protect something from a pest

7. Causing injury to plant life

8. Surroundings, usually water, air, soil, plants and animals

9. Any plant or plant part, animal or animal product produced by a person

10. United States Environmental Protection Agency

A. Private applicator
B. Pesticide
C. Tolerance
D. Agricultural commodity
E. Certification
F. Environment
G. Exposure
H. Phytotoxicity
I. Hazard
J. EPA

1._____
2._____
3._____
4._____
5._____
6._____
7._____
8._____
9._____
10._____

45

Questions 11-28

11. Any living thing	A. Pest	11._____
12. Harmful condition which affects plant life	B. Insect	12._____
13. Unwanted organism	C. Mite, tick and spider	13._____
14. Organism that lives and feeds in or on another organism	D. Plant disease	14._____
	E. Nematode	
15. Small invertebrate animal with three body regions and six jointed legs; may have two, four or no wings	F. Parasite	15._____
	G. Life cycle	
16. One-celled microorganism which causes wilts, cankers and other plant diseases	H. Larva	16._____
17. Immature stage of an insect that does not look like an adult insect	I. Pupa	17._____
	J. Nymph	
18. Immature stage of an insect that looks similar to an adult insect	K. Organism	18._____
19. Small roundworm that feeds on or in plants and animals	L. Fungus	19._____
	M. Bacterium	
20. Signal that something is wrong in a plant, such as change in growth habits	N. Annual	20._____
21. Plant that grows two years, produces seed and then dies	O. Symptom or sign	21._____
	P. Vertebrate	
22. Stages in the life development of organisms	Q. Perennial	22._____
23. Nonfeeding, usually immobile stage of an insect before becoming an adult	R. Biennial	23._____
24. Animals closely related to insects but with with two body regions, eight jointed legs and no wings		24._____
25. Plant that normally lives for more than two years		25._____
26. Small plant which causes rot, mold and other plant diseases		26._____
27. Animal with a bony spinal column		27._____
28. Plant that grows from seed, produces seed the same year and dies		28._____

Questions 29-36

29. Amount of pesticide that remains on or in a crop or animal or on a surface following application

30. Movement of pesticide droplets or particles by wind and air currents

31. Way of describing how all animals depend on others for food

32. Area, building, animal, plant or pest intended to be treated with pesticide

33. Causing injury to plant life; poisonous to plant life

34. Study of the relationship between a plant or animal and its surroundings

35. Surroundings such as water, air, soil, plants and animals

36. Process of becoming a gas

A. Residue
B. Phytotoxicity
C. Target
D. Ecology
E. Drift
F. Environment
G. Food chain or web
H. Vaporization

29._____
30._____
31._____
32._____
33._____
34._____
35._____
36._____

Questions 37-40

37. Pesticide that stays in the environment for a rather long period of time

38. Pesticide that does not collect and build up in the body of an animal or plant even when the animal or plant is repeatedly exposed

39. Pesticide that can collect and build up in the body of an animal or plant when the animal or plant is repeatedly exposed

40. Pesticide that does not stay in the environment for a long period of time

A. Accumulative
B. Persistent
C. Nonaccumulative
D. Nonpersistent

37._____
38._____
39._____
40._____

Questions 41-66

41. Chemical or other substance that will destroy or control a pest or protect something from a pest

42. Pesticide which kills when swallowed

43. Pesticide that is taken up by one part of a plant or animal and moved to another section where it acts against a pest

44. Pesticide that breaks down almost immediately into non-toxic byproducts

45. Pesticide which enters the pest in the form of a gas and kills it

46. Pesticide that remains in the environment for a fairly long time

47. Pesticide spray which is evenly applied to the outside of the object to be protected

48. Pesticide which kills when it touches or is touched by the pest

49. Pesticide applied before pests are actually found but where they are expected

50. Pesticide which kills the pest after it appears

51. Pesticide used before the crop is planted

52. Pesticide used before crop or weeds appear; may also refer to use after crop emerges or is established but before weeds emerge

53. Pesticide used after crop or weeds have appeared

54. Pesticide which draws moisture from or dries up a plant, plant part or insect causing it to die

55. Pesticide which causes the leaves of a plant to drop off

56. Pesticide used to control insects

57. Chemical which coats the leaves of plants to reduce water loss

A. Short-term (non-persistent)
B. Stomach poison
C. Pesticide
D. Eradicant
E. Preplant
F. Residual (persistent)
G. Systemic
H. Surface spray
I. Contact poison
J. Protectant (preventive)
K. Preemergence
L. Fumigant poison
M. Postemergence
N. Fungicide
O. Herbicide
P. Desiccant
Q. Defoliant
R. Rodenticide
S. Insecticide
T. Antitranspirant
U. Nematicide
V. Growth regulator
W. Miticide
X. Nonselective
Y. Selective
Z. Broad spectrum

41._____
42._____
43._____
44._____
45._____
46._____
47._____
48._____
49._____
50._____
51._____
52._____
53._____
54._____
55._____
56._____
57._____

58. Pesticide which increases, decreases or changes the normal growth of a plant   58._____

59. Pesticide used to control unwanted plants   59._____

60. Pesticide used to control fungi which cause molds, rots and other plant diseases   60._____

61. Pesticide used to control rodents such as rats and mice   61._____

62. Pesticide used to control nematodes   62._____

63. Pesticide used to control mites   63._____

64. Pesticide which is toxic to a wide range of pests; used when several different pests are a problem   64._____

65. Pesticide which is toxic to all or most plants or animals of a type; usually used to describe a particular type of pesticide   65._____

66. Pesticide which is more toxic to some types of plants or animals than to others; usually used to describe a particular type of pesticide   66._____

Questions 67-70

67. Used as a bait, surface spray or dust; must be eaten by the pest

A. Fumigant poison   67._____

B. Contact poison

68. Used as a surface spray, dust or in soil incorporation; must touch or be touched by the pest   68._____

C. Systemic poison

D. Stomach poison

69. Used as a surface or foliar spray, pour-on, injection or granule   69._____

70. Applied as a gas or as a liquid which then vaporizes   70._____

KEY (CORRECT ANSWERS)

1. C	11. K	21. R	31. G	41. C	51. E	61. R
2. E	12. D	22. G	32. C	42. B	52. K	62. U
3. G	13. A	23. I	33. B	43. G	53. M	63. W
4. I	14. F	24. C	34. D	44. A	54. P	64. X/Z
5. A	15. B	25. Q	35. F	45. L	55. Q	65. X/Z
6. B	16. M	26. L	36. H	46. F	56. S	66. Y
7. H	17. H	27. P	37. B	47. H	57. T	67. D
8. F	18. J	28. N	38. C	48. I	58. V	68. B
9. D	19. E	29. A	39. A	49. J	59. O	69. C
10. J	20. O	30. E	40. D	50. D	60. N	70. A

TEST 2

DIRECTIONS: Read the statements and descriptions listed in the column to the left and match each with the correct term or phrase from the list to the right. *PRINT THE LETTER OF THE CORRECT ANSWER IN THE SPACE AT THE RIGHT.*

Questions 1-7

1. Used where other control methods would not provide the needed control
2. Includes quarantines, inspections, embargoes and compulsory crop or product destruction
3. Removing the source of food or nest site will aid in getting rid of pests
4. Traps, barriers, light, sound, heat, cold, radiation and electrocution are all used to remove or keep the pests from the area where they are not wanted
5. Planting, growing, harvesting and tillage practices may help or harm pests
6. Natural enemies such as parasites, predators and disease agents are used to control pests, especially insects, mites and some weeds
7. Choosing crops, animals and lumber which resist or are unharmed by pests

A. Pesticide
B. Biological control
C. Legal control
D. Cultural control
E. Sanitation
F. Mechanical-physical control
G. Resistant variety

1._____
2._____
3._____
4._____
5._____
6._____
7._____

Questions 8-16

8. Poisonous; ability to cause injury to plants and animals, including humans
9. Technical information including the label and any other printed material provided by the manufacturer or its agent to accompany a pesticide product
10. Chemical or other substance that can cause injury or death when eaten, absorbed or inhaled by plants or animals, including man

A. Label
B. Signal words
C. Pesticide
D. Pest
E. Active ingredient
F. Toxic

8._____
9._____
10._____

11. Words which must appear on pesticide labels to show toxicity of pesticide

12. Written material attached to or printed on a pesticide container or wrapper

13. Unwanted organism

14. Chemical or other substance that will prevent, repel, destroy or control a pest or protect something from a pest

15. That part of a pesticide product which will kill or control pests or prevent damage by them

16. Period of time between a pesticide application and when workers may go back into an area without wearing protective clothing or equipment

G. Labeling
H. Poison
I. Reentry

11._____
12._____
13._____
14._____
15._____
16._____

Questions 17-22

17. Use labels to control sale, use, safety, storage and disposal of pesticides

18. Use labels as the license to sell a pesticide

19. Use labels to determine the antidote to use in the proper treatment of poisoning cases

20. Use labels as a way of deciding which pesticide will be effective against the pest and be the safest to use

21. Use labels to decide what safety precautions to take and how much pesticide to use

22. Use labels to aid in making recommendations to buyers and users

A. State and federal governments
B. Manufacturers of pesticides
C. Dealers and pest control experts
D. Buyers and users
E. Physicians

17._____
18._____
19._____
20._____
21._____
22._____

Questions 23-25

23. Well-known, made-up name accepted by the Environmental Protection Agency to identify the active ingredients in a pesticide

24. Scientific "often complicated" name which tells what the active ingredients are

25. Name used by a manufacturer to identify a pesticide as their product

A. Brand name
B. Common name
C. Chemical name

23._____
24._____
25._____

Questions 26-28

26. Highly toxic pesticides; the word *poison* printed in red and the skull and crossbones symbol are also required on labels of highly toxic pesticides

27. Slightly toxic to relatively non-toxic pesticides

28. Moderately toxic pesticides

A. Caution
B. Warning
C. Danger

26._____
27._____
28._____

Questions 29-47

29. Treatment given by a medically trained person to reduce the effects of pesticide poisoning

30. Through the mouth

31. Matter which is vomited

32. To take a pesticide or other material into a plant, animal or the soil

33. How poisonous a pesticide is to a living organism

34. Deadly

35. Severe reaction of the human body to a serious injury; can result in death if not treated

A. Inhalation
B. Inhalation toxicity
C. LC_{50}
D. LD_{50}
E. Lethal
F. Oral
G. Vomitus
H. Shock
I. Signs/symptoms
J. Toxicity

29._____
30._____
31._____
32._____
33._____
34._____
35._____

36. Poisoning which occurs after a single exposure to a pesticide

37. Dose or amount of a pesticide which would kill half of a large number of test animals if eaten or absorbed through the skin

38. Poisoning which occurs as a result of repeated exposures to pesticides over a period of time

39. Concentration of a pesticide in the air which would kill half of a large number of test animals exposed to it

40. To touch or be touched by

41. How poisonous a pesticide is to man or animal when breathed in through the lungs

42. How poisonous a pesticide is to man or animal when in contact with the skin

43. Risk of danger; chance that injury or harm will come to the applicator, other persons, plants or animals

44. To take air into the lungs; to breathe in

45. To make a pesticide thinner or weaker by adding water, oil or other material; to water down

46. First effort to help a victim of poisoning while medical help is on the way

47. Warning that something is wrong

K. Antidote
L. Dilute
M. Absorb
N. Dermal toxicity
O. Acute poisoning
P. Contact
Q. Chronic poisoning
R. First aid
S. Hazard

36._____
37._____
38._____
39._____
40._____
41._____
42._____
43._____
44._____
45._____
46._____
47._____

Questions 48-56

48. Used as a drinking glass or for collecting vomitus

49. Used to wash pesticides quickly off the skin

50. Used for emergency phone calls

51. Used to induce vomiting and to aid a person in shock

A. Bag of activated charcoal
B. Plastic bottle of detergent
C. Clean, empty jar
D. Shaped plastic airway

48._____
49._____
50._____
51._____

52. Used for covering a victim
53. Used for wrapping cuts and scrapes and for protecting burns
54. Used for diluting the salt
55. Used for mouth-to-mouth resuscitation
56. When mixed with water and swallowed, acts as an absorber of all pesticides

E. Plastic container of salt
F. Coins
G. Plastic bottle of water
H. Band-aids, bandages and tape
I. Blanket

52._____
53._____
54._____
55._____
56._____

Questions 57-72

57. Process of directing or placing pesticides on or in plants, animals, buildings, soil, air, water or other site
58. Metal or plastic container filled with absorbent materials to filter fumes and vapors from the air
59. Cylinder-shaped part of the respirator which absorbs fumes and vapors from the air
60. Portion or amount of pesticide mixture which is directed at the target
61. Pest to be treated with a pesticide
62. Direction toward which the prevailing wind is blowing
63. Face mask which filters out poisonous gases and particles
64. Movement by wind and air currents of droplets or particles of a pesticide
65. Period of time between a pesticide application and when persons may reenter an area without wearing protective clothing and equipment
66. To make unclean or unsafe
67. Surroundings, usually water, air, soil, plants and animals
68. A kind of synthetic rubber

A. Target
B. Respirator
C. Reentry interval
D. Pollute
E. Cannister
F. Fume
G. Face shield
H. Vaporize
I. Environment
J. Drift
K. Downwind
L. Dose, dosage
M. Cartridge
N. Application
O. Neoprene
P. Exposure

57._____
58._____
59._____
60._____
61._____
62._____
63._____
64._____
65._____
66._____
67._____
68._____

69. To form a gas and disappear into the air 69._____

70. Not protected or shielded; contact with pesticides through mouth, lungs or skin 70._____

71. Piece of protective equipment used by pesticide applicator to protect face from exposure 71._____

72. Unpleasant or irritating smoke, vapor or gas 72._____

KEY (CORRECT ANSWERS)

1. A	11. B	21. D	31. G	41. B	51. E	61. A	71. G
2. C	12. A	22. C	32. M	42. N	52. I	62. K	72. F
3. E	13. D	23. B	33. J	43. S	53. H	63. B	
4. F	14. C	24. C	34. E	44. A	54. G	64. J	
5. D	15. E	25. A	35. H	45. L	55. D	65. C	
6. B	16. I	26. C	36. O	46. R	56. A	66. D	
7. G	17. A	27. A	37. D	47. I	57. N	67. I	
8. F	18. B	28. B	38. Q	48. C	58. E	68. O	
9. G	19. E	29. K	39. C	49. B	59. M	69. H	
10. H	20. D	30. F	40. P	50. F	60. L	70. P	

TEST 3

DIRECTIONS: Read the statements and descriptions listed in the column to the left and match each with the correct term or phrase from the list to the right. *PRINT THE LETTER OF THE CORRECT ANSWER IN THE SPACE AT THE RIGHT.*

Questions 1-7

1. Area, building, plant or animal to be treated with pesticide in order to protect it from or reach the target pest

2. Pesticide as it is sold before diluting; usually contains a large amount of active ingredient

3. Pest to be controlled with a pesticide

4. Mixture of one or more active ingredients with other materials needed to make a pesticide easy to store, handle, dilute and apply

5. Able to be combined with other pesticides and applied as a mixture without reducing their effectiveness

6. Mixture made by dissolving a substance in a liquid; mixture will not separate or settle out in normal use

7. Liquid such as water, kerosene or alcohol that a pesticide or other substance will dissolve in and form a solution

A. Formulation
B. Target
C. Site
D. Compatible
E. Concentrate
F. Solvent
G. Solution

1._____
2._____
3._____
4._____
5._____
6._____
7._____

Questions 8-17

8. Dry preparation which may contain a fairly high concentration (15-95%) of active ingredient and is mixed with water to form a suspension when applied

9. Dry preparation which contains a fairly high concentration of active ingredient that dissolves in water to form a solution for application

10. Active ingredient in the form of a gas or liquid which becomes a gas when applied and reaches the target as a gas

11. Finely ground, ready-to-use dry mixture combining a small amount of active ingredient with an inert carrier such as talc, clay or volcanic ash

12. Very finely ground solid material which is suspended in a liquid; usually contains a high concentration or large amount of the active ingredient and is mixed with water when applied

13. Food or other attractive substance mixed with an active ingredient that will attract and be eaten by pests and cause death

14. Ready-to-use dry mixture of a small amount of active ingredient and inert carriers with all particles larger than dust particles

15. Solution which may contain pure active ingredient; usually used without dilution

16. Solution which contains a high concentration or large amount of active ingredient which should be mixed with water; may contain from one to several pounds of active ingredient per gallon of concentrate

17. Solution which contains a low concentration or small amount of active ingredient in a highly refined oil or other solvent

A. Dust (D)
B. Fumigant
C. Wettable powder (WP or W)
D. Soluble powder (SP)
E. Emulsifiable concentrate solution (EC or E)
F. Ultra-low volume concentrate solution (ULV)
G. Flowable (F)
H. Granule (G)
I. Low concentrate solution (S)
J. Poisonous bait (B)

8. _____
9. _____
10. _____
11. _____
12. _____
13. _____
14. _____
15. _____
16. _____
17. _____

Questions 18-29

18. Complete or partial immersion of a plant, animal or object in a pesticide
19. Application to a small area
20. Aiming the pesticide at a portion of a plant, animal or structure
21. Application to the soil followed by use of tillage implements to mix the pesticide with the soil
22. Saturation of the soil with a pesticide or oral treatment of an animal
23. Application along the side of a crop row
24. Application to the leaves of a plant, shrub or tree
25. Pouring the pesticide along the midline of the backs of livestock
26. Application to a strip or band over or along each crop row
27. Application over the top of the growing plant
28. Uniform application to an entire specified area
29. Application to or in a furrow in which a crop is planted

A. Band
B. Broadcast
C. Dip
D. Directed
E. Drench
F. Foliar
G. In-furrow
H. Over-the-top
I. Pour-on
J. Sidedress
K. Soil incorporation
L. Spot treatment

18.____
19.____
20.____
21.____
22.____
23.____
24.____
25.____
26.____
27.____
28.____
29.____

Questions 30-36

30. Circular pattern; used for spraying foliage
31. Wide flat fan pattern; used for boomless sprayers or to extend the effective width on the end of the boom
32. Uniform pattern across its width; used for band spraying
33. Circular pattern with little or no spray in the center; used for spraying foliage
34. Wide angle spray pattern; used for broadcast spraying

A. Broadcast
B. Flooding flat fan
C. Hollow cone
D. Solid (full) cone
E. Solid stream
F. Regular flat fan
G. Even flat fan

30.____
31.____
32.____
33.____
34.____

4 (#3)

35. Narrow oval pattern with lighter edges; used for broadcast spraying

35._____

36. Compact jet used in handguns to spray a distant target or fixed to apply a narrow band or to inject into the soil

36._____

Questions 37-48

37. Easily injured

A. Soil injection

37._____

38. Act or process of correctly discarding pesticides and pesticide containers; can include recycling, deposit-return, reuse or burning

B. Monitoring system

38._____

C. Original container

D. Pollute

39. Pollute or make unfit for use

39._____

E. Diluent

40. Side toward which the prevailing wind blows

40._____

F. Contaminate

41. Liquid, such as water, kerosene, alcohol or dust, which waters down or weakens a concentrated pesticide

G. Sensitive

41._____

H. Disposal

42. Method of disposal of pesticides and pesticide containers by sealing them in sturdy, waterproof, chemical-proof containers which are then sealed in thick plastic, steel or concrete to resist damage or breakage

42._____

I. Downwind

J. Encapsulation

K. Herbicide

43. To make unclean or unsafe

43._____

L. Incinerator

44. Pesticide that is used to control unwanted plants

44._____

45. Package (bag, can or bottle) in which a pesticide is sold

45._____

46. Special high-heat furnace or burner which reduces everything to nontoxic ash and gas

46._____

47. Regular system of keeping track of and checking up on whether or not pesticides are escaping into the environment

47._____

48. Method of disposal of pesticides by putting them within the plow layer of soil by usual tillage practices

48._____

KEY (CORRECT ANSWERS)

1. C	11. A	21. K	31. A	41. E
2. E	12. G	22. E	32. G	42. J
3. B	13. J	23. J	33. C	43. D
4. A	14. H	24. F	34. B	44. K
5. D	15. F	25. I	35. F	45. C
6. G	16. E	26. A	36. E	46. L
7. F	17. I	27. H	37. G	47. B
8. C	18. C	28. B	38. H	48. A
9. D	19. L	29. G	39. F	
10. B	20. D	30. D	40. I	

PESTICIDES

TERMS AND DEFINITIONS

GENERAL

Private applicator — A certified applicator who uses or supervises the use of any pesticide classified for restricted use for the purpose of producing any agricultural commodity on the property owned or rented by him or his employer or on the property of another person producing any agricultural commodity in exchange of personal services

Pesticide — Chemical or other substance that will prevent, repel, destroy or control a pest or protect something from a pest

Tolerance — Maximum amount of pesticide which can legally remain on or in any food or feed crop at harvest or animal at slaughter

Agricultural Commodity — Any plant or plant part, animal or animal product produced by a person

Certification — Recognition by certifying agency that a person is competent and thus authorized to use or supervise the use of restricted-use pesticides

Environment — Surroundings, usually water, air, soil, plants and animals

Exposure — Not protected or shielded; contact with pesticide through ingestion, inhalation or skin contact

Phytotoxicity — Causing injury to plant life

Hazard — Risk of danger; chance that injury or harm will come to the applicator, other persons, plants or animals

EPA — United States Environmental Protection Agency

PESTS

Organism — Any living thing

Pest — Unwanted organism

Vertebrate — Animal with a bony spinal column

Insect — Small invertebrate animal with three body regions and six jointed legs; may have two, four or no wings

Mite, tick, spider — Animals closely related to insects but with two body regions, eight jointed legs and no wings

Plant disease	Harmful condition which affects plant life
Nematode	Small roundworm that feeds on or in plants and animals
Parasite	Organism that lives and feeds in or on another organism
Life cycle	Stages in the life development of organisms
Larva	Immature stage of an insect that does not look like an adult insect
Pupa	Nonfeeding, usually immobile stage of an insect before becoming an adult
Nymph	Immature stage of an insect that looks similar to an adult insect
Fungus	Small plant which causes rot, mold and other plant diseases (plural: fungi)
Bacterium	One-celled microorganism which causes wilts, cankers and other plant diseases (plural: bacteria)
Disease symptom	Signal that something is wrong in a plant, such as change in growth habits
Annual	Plant that grows from seed, produces seed the same year and then dies
Perennial	Plant that normally lives for more than two years
Biennial	Plant that grows two years, produces seed and then dies

ENVIRONMENTAL PROTECTION

Ecology	Study of the relationship between a plant or animal and its surroundings
Food chain/web	Way of describing how all animals depend on others for food; the relationship among plants, plant eaters and meat eaters
Vaporization	Process of becoming a gas
Drift	Movement of pesticide droplets or particles by wind or air currents
Target	Area, building, plant, animal or pest intended to be treated with pesticide
Residue	Amount of pesticide that remains on or in a crop or animal or on a surface following application

PESTICIDES

Stomach poison — Pesticide which kills when swallowed

Fumigant poison — Pesticide which enters the pest in the form of a gas and kills it

Contact poison — Pesticide which kills when it touches or is touched by the pest

Systemic — Pesticide that is taken up by one part of a plant or animal and moved to another section where it acts against a pest

Short-term (nonpersistent) — Pesticide that breaks down almost immediately into nontoxic byproducts

Residual (persistent) — Pesticide that remains in the environment for a fairly long time

Broad spectrum (non-selective) — Pesticide which is toxic to a wide range of pests; used when several different pests are a problem (*short term, residual* and *broad spectrum* are often used in describing insecticides and miticides)

Surface spray — Pesticide spray which is evenly applied to the outside of the object to be protected

Selective — Pesticide which is more toxic to some types of plants or animals than to others; usually used to describe a particular type of pesticide (ex. a selective herbicide would kill crabgrass in a cornfield but would not injure the corn)

Nonselective — Pesticide which is toxic to all or most plants or animals of a type; usually used to describe a particular type of pesticide (ex. A nonselective herbicide would kill or injure all plant sin the application site but not all insects, animals or other organisms)

Protectant (preventive) — Pesticide applied before pests are actually found but where they are expected

Eradicant — Pesticide which kills the pest before it appears

Preplant — Pesticide used before the crop is planted

Preemergence — Pesticide used before crop or weeds appear; may also refer to use after crop emerges or is established but before weeds emerge

Postemergence — Pesticide used after crop or weeds have appeared

Desiccant — Pesticide which draws moisture from or dries up a plant, plant part or insect causing it to die

Defoliant	Pesticide which causes the leaves of a plant to drop off
Antitranspirant	Chemical which coats the leaves of plants to reduce water loss
Growth regulator	Pesticide which increases, decreases or changes the normal growth of a plant
Herbicide	Pesticide used to control unwanted plants
Fungicide	Pesticide used to control fungi which cause molds, rots and other plant diseases
Rodenticide	Pesticide used to control rodents such as rats and mice
Nematicide	Pesticides used to control nematodes
Miticide	Pesticides used to control mites
Insecticide	Pesticides used to control insects

LABELS AND LABELING

Active Ingredient	That part of a pesticide product which will kill or control pests or prevent damage by them; the actual poison in a product
Label	Written material attached to or printed on a pesticide container or wrapper
Labeling	Technical information including the label and any other printed material provided by the manufacturer or its agent to accompany a pesticide product
Poison	Chemical or other substance that can cause injury or death when eaten, absorbed or inhaled by plants or animals, including man
Signal words	Words which must appear on pesticide labels to show toxicity of pesticide
Toxic	Poisonous; ability to cause injury to plants or animals, including humans
Reentry	Period of time between a pesticide application and when workers may go back into an area without wearing protective clothing or equipment

PERSONAL SAFETY AND FIRST AID

Antidote	Treatment given by a medically trained person to reduce the effects of pesticide poisoning

Absorb	To take a pesticide or other material into a plant, animal or the soil
Acute poisoning	Poisoning which occurs after a single exposure to a pesticide
Chronic poisoning	Poisoning which occurs as a result of repeated exposures to pesticides over a period of time
Contact	To touch or be touched by
Dermal toxicity	How poisonous a pesticide is to man or animal when in contact with the skin
Dilute	To make a pesticide thinner or weaker by adding water, oil or other material; to water down
First aid	First effort to help a victim of poisoning while medical help is on the way
Hazard	Risk of danger; chance that injury or harm will come to the applicator, other persons, plants or animals
Inhalation	To take air into the lungs; to breathe in
Inhalation toxicity	How poisonous a pesticide is to man or animal when breathed in through the lungs
LC_{50}	Concentration of a pesticide in the air which would kill half of a large number of test animals exposed to it (The lower the LC number value, the more poisonous the pesticide. It is often used as the measure of acute inhalation toxicity. LC stands for lethal concentration.)
LD_{50}	Dose or amount of a pesticide which would kill half of a large number of test animals if eaten or absorbed through the skin (The lower the LD number value, the more poisonous the pesticide. LD number values are the commonly used measures of acute oral or acute dermal toxicity. LD stands for lethal dose.)
Lethal	Deadly
Oral	Through the mouth
Shock	Severe reaction of the human body to a serious injury; can result in death if not treated
Signs/symptoms	Warning that something is wrong. (A sign is an outward signal of a disease or poisoning in a plant or animal, including humans. A symptom is a feeling of being sick.)
Toxicity	How poisonous a pesticide is to a living organism
Vomitus	Matter which is vomited

SAFETY BEFORE, DURING AND FOLLOWING APPLICATION

Application	Process of directing or placing pesticides on or in plants, animals, buildings, soil, air, water or other site
Cartridge	Cylinder-shaped part of the respirator which absorbs fumes and vapors from the air
Cannister	Metal or plastic container filled with absorbent materials to filter fumes and vapors from the air
Dose/dosage	Portion or amount of pesticide mixture which is directed at the target
Downwind	Direction toward which the prevailing wind is blowing
Drift	Movement by wind and air currents of droplets or particles of a pesticide
Vaporize	To form a gas and disappear into the air
Face shield	Piece of protective equipment used by a pesticide applicator to protect face from exposure
Fume	Unpleasant or irritating smoke, vapor or gas
Neoprene	A kind of synthetic rubber
Pollute	To make unclean or unsafe
Respirator	Face mask which filters out poisonous gases and particles; used to protect the nose, mouth and lungs from pesticide injury

FORMULATION AND APPLICATION

Formulation	Mixture of one or more active ingredients with other materials needed to make a pesticide easy to store, handle, dilute and apply
Site	Area, building, plant or animal to be treated with pesticide in order to protect it from or reach the target pest
Compatible	Able to be combined with other pesticides and applied as a mixture without reducing their effectiveness
Concentrate	Pesticide as it is sold before diluting; usually contains a large amount of active ingredient
Solvent	Liquid such as water, kerosene or alcohol that a pesticide or other substance will dissolve in and form a solution

Solution	Mixture made by dissolving a substance in a liquid; mixture will not separate or settle out in normal use

EQUIPMENT AND ITS USE

Dilute	To make a pesticide thinner or weaker by adding water, oil or other materials
Diluent	Liquid or dust used to water down or weaken a concentrated pesticide
Adjuvant (additive)	Substance added to the pesticide formulation or tank mix to make the active ingredient work better (ex. wetting agent, spreaders, adhesive, emulsifying agent, penetrant)
Calibration	Measurement of how much pesticide will be applied by the equipment to the site; measurement of the daily rate

DISPOSAL AND STORAGE

Disposal	Act or process of correctly discarding pesticides and pesticide containers; can include recycling, deposit-return, reuse or burning
Downwind	Side towards which the prevailing wind is blowing
Encapsulation	Method of disposal of pesticides and pesticide containers by sealing them in sturdy, waterproof, chemical-proof container which is then sealed in thick plastic, steel or concrete to resist damage or breakage
Incinerator	Special high-heat furnace or burner which reduces everything to nontoxic ash and gas
Soil injection	Method of disposal of pesticides by putting them within the plow layer of soil by usual tillage practices
Monitoring system	Regular system of keeping track of and checking up on whether or not pesticides are escaping into the environment
Original container	Package in which a pesticide is sold (the package must have a label telling what the pesticide is, how to use it correctly and safely, and how to safely dispose of the empty container)
Pollute	To make unclean or unsafe
Contaminate	Pollute or make unfit for use
Sensitive	Easily injured

PESTICIDE HANDLING CHECKLIST

Everyone can improve his methods of handling pesticides. Each year many accidents occur because of improper and careless handling of pesticides. How do you stand? Are you following safe practices? Check yourself by answering the following questions. Remember that one "No" answer may be what gets you in trouble.

STORE YOUR PESTICIDES SAFELY   <u>YES</u>   <u>NO</u>

Do you have a separate space to store pesticides?

Do you keep it locked and are the windows tight, barred or boarded over?

Do you keep all your pesticides in this storage rather than in the garage, feed room, basement, porch, kitchen or refrigerator?

Do you store herbicides separately from other pesticides?

Are there signs on your storage so firemen and others are warned?

Do you check periodically for leaking containers?

KEEP IN THE ORIGINAL CONTAINER SO THE LABEL IS THERE!

Do you always keep pesticides in the original container instead of old "coke" bottles, milk cartons or other food containers?

When people ask you for a little spray mix out of your tank, do you refuse?

Do you always remember what is in an unlabeled container?

Do you always remember the safety precautions, antidotes and directions for use, even though the container is not labeled?

Do you safely dispose of unlabeled pesticides, rather than take a chance with your memory?

USE THE RECOMMENDED CLOTHING AND PROTECTIVE EQUIPMENT

Do you read the label to see what protective clothing you should wear?

	YES	NO

Do you start each spraying day with clean spray clothing?

Do you check the signal word and precautions for use on the label to see what protective equipment is necessary?

Do you wear the protective equipment recommended on the label?

Do you clean and maintain your protective equipment regularly and often?

Do you throw away rubber gloves that have only tiny holes in them?

SPILLS AND SPLASHES OF CONCENTRATE CAN BE VERY HAZARDOUS!

Do you know what to do if you should spill a pesticide on yourself while mixing?

Do you wear adequate footgear with your pant cuffs on the outside so pesticides won't run into your footgear?

Do you have sawdust, vermiculite, kitty litter or some other absorbent on hand to soak up spills?

Do you always watch your sprayer tank when filling so it won't run over and spill on the ground?

Do you have a check valve or other device on your equipment to prevent back-siphoning into the water supply?

Is your application equipment well maintained so it doesn't leak and leave toxic puddles or piles of pesticide on the ground?

Do you avoid draining leftover spray mix on the ground?

Do you discard old high-pressure hose instead of patching it and hoping no one will be nearby when it bursts?

Do you clean nozzles with a brush or by rinsing instead of blowing them out with your mouth?

	YES	NO

POOR CONTAINER DISPOSAL MAY CAUSE BAD ACCIDENTS!

<u>YES</u>   <u>NO</u>

Do you rinse each "empty" liquid container at least three times and dump the rinsings into the tank?

Do you keep your used containers in your storage area until disposed?

Do you collect every container for disposal before leaving a job instead of leaving them in the field or at your tank filling station?

Do you puncture, break or crush nonburnable containers so they can't be reused?

Do you keep or return to the manufacturer 30- and 55-gallon pesticide drums, rather than giving them away for floats or trash barrels?

ATTRACTIVE NUISANCES CAN RESULT IN LAWSUITS!

Do you keep your spray equipment where children cannot play on it?

Do you keep your spray equipment clean so that those touching it will not be contaminated?

Do you always release pressure on your equipment so spray guns won't accidentally be triggered?

CARE IN APPLICATION PREVENTS ACCIDENTS

Do you check the wind direction and the area downwind before applying pesticides?

Do you consider substituting a safer chemical if you are spraying near a sensitive area?

Do you check for the possibility of showers and damaging runoff before applying pesticides?

Do you plan your pesticide application so it will have little or no effect on bees, birds, fish or other wildlife?

Do you remove, turn over or cover pet dishes, sand boxes and plastic pools before spraying private property?

Do you make sure that children and pets are out of the area and stay out until the spray dries?

Do you use the least toxic pesticide that will control the known pest, if all other factors are equal?

www.ingramcontent.com/pod-product-compliance
Lightning Source LLC
Chambersburg PA
CBHW082214300426
44117CB00016B/2799